THE CINEMA OF ANDREI TARKOVSKY

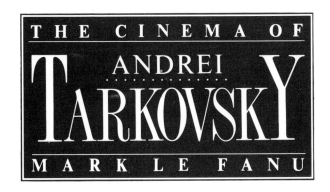

THE CINEMA OF
ANDREI
TARKOVSKY

MARK LE FANU

BFI PUBLISHING

First published in 1987 by the British Film Institute
21 Stephen Street
London W1P 1PL
Reprinted 1990

British Library Cataloguing in Publication Data

Le Fanu, Mark, 1950–
    The cinema of Andrei Tarkovsky.
    1. Tarskovskii, Andrei
    I. Title
    791.43'0233'0924   PN1998.A3T282

    ISBN 0-85170-193-0
    ISBN 0-85170-194-9 Pbk

Set in Imprint
Cover design: Geoff Wiggins

Typeset by W. S. Cowell Ltd., Ipswich, Suffolk
and printed by Courier International, Tiptree, Essex

CONTENTS

Preface and acknowledgments

I have never believed that a critic's task is primarily hermeneutic. If Tarkovsky is a difficult artist in some ways, the response as I see it should be for the critic to try to place his work in as wide and sympathetic a cultural context as possible. The focus here is not 'Russian Studies', about which, alas, I am unqualified to speak, but – as this book's publishing provenance suggests – the classical cinema. I am writing this short book for the person who is interested in Tarkovsky and the Russian cinema, and in Tarkovsky's relation to Western film-makers. So Bergman, Buñuel, Kurosawa, Antonioni and other great names from the 50s and 60s are a certain point of reference; Tarkovsky knew and loved their work, and learnt from it, as he did from the old Russian masters.

A word may be said about my method. I have used throughout the *auteurist* convention of writing about films as if they were the product of a single mind, when in fact everyone knows they are collaborative exercises. The best film books these days will tend to have extensive interviews with screenwriters, cameramen, set designers and numerous other people whose creative 'input' counts in the overall artefact. I have not gone along with this for various reasons. The *auteur* theory is not purely myth: its categories need to be deepened, not abolished. In the end, some one individual is responsible for the work in question, and (especially in a book about Tarkovsky) I couldn't wish to part from conventional wisdom in believing that it's the director.

Tarkovsky is a film-maker whom people tend either to like or dislike rather strongly. It has been my good fortune during the writing of this book to have spent many pleasant evenings with people who like his films and feel deeply about him. The discussion of Tarkovsky's films was in several cases the making of a friendship. I should mention conversations with Tim and Stephen Quay, John Gillett, Keith Griffiths, Irina Brown, Alain Passes, David Thompson, Andrzej Krauze and Malgosia Pióro (always a hospitable hearth and good company with these two), Tamara Follini, Lys Flowerday, Rosemary Morton; also Andrzej and Danusia Klimowski, Witek and Danusia Stock. Peter and Natasha Norman were kindness itself in the early stages of my researches.

John Raish lent me his house in Greece for a crucial period. Donatella Baglivo was hospitable in Rome. Irina Shumovich provided me throughout with some excellent translations. I must especially thank Layla Alexander for her patience and understanding in relaying my enquiries to Tarkovsky. Christopher Silvester read a first draft of the manuscript and made many helpful suggestions, as did Kitty Hunter Blair a second. (Errors and misreadings that remain are the author's responsibility.) In the latter stages of my project the Leverhulme Trust gave me a small grant for travel expenses, and I must thank the Trustees and their secretary Miss J. E. Bennett for this kindness.

Stills by National Film Archive, London. Acknowledgment is made to the distributors of Tarkovsky's films, and to *Sight and Sound*.

TARKOVSKY AND RUSSIAN CINEMA

Between 1962 and 1979 Andrei Tarkovsky directed five major films in Russia – a film every three or four years. (In the West, Stanley Kubrick, similarly perfectionist, makes a film about every six years.) A number of these films – *Andrei Roublev* most notably – found themselves held back on their completion, but all of them were eventually shown to domestic audiences, as well as being exported.

Tarkovsky's position in Russia, therefore, was already different from that of the older generation of artists like Pasternak, not to mention obviously dissident writers like Sinyavsky or Solzhenitsyn. We wonder how this came to be so. The great, until recently banned novel, *Doctor Zhivago* is explicit in its admiration for the Christianity which Lenin never quite succeeded in eradicating. But so, unmistakably, is *Andrei Roublev*. Why should such a message be thought subversive in Pasternak's case, but in Tarkovsky's case apparently not?

Very complicated issues are at stake here: differences between literary and cinematic culture, as well as hard to track down intrigues between organisations and individuals. If we wish, though, we may hazard a few guesses. Firstly, the spiritual climate was significantly different between 1956, when Pasternak first submitted his manuscript, and 1962, when Tarkovsky proposed his historical epic. Then, again, Pasternak's sceptical Christian melancholy, adumbrated in the context of a twentieth-century drama (showing the results of the Russian revolution), could rather too obviously be read as a philosophical criticism of Communism; whereas with *Andrei Roublev* this is ostensibly not the case. Roublev the fifteenth-century icon painter was, in a certain sense, a patriotic figure, to whom the authorities themselves in 1960 had dedicated a sexcentenary exhibition. The 'barbarism' of the times could be explained in terms of orthodox Marxism. The film would be mainly one of 'spectacle'. These, and like considerations, may have persuaded the authorities that it was safe to let the young director (32 in 1964) make a go of his script.

In the event, of course, Tarkovsky's film did run into opposition. And it is proper to remind ourselves that this great epic only barely made it to the screen. So the question remains: how, having made this film, was Tarkovsky allowed to go on to make four other films? Why wasn't he silenced (or edged out, made unemployable) at that moment in the late 1960s when the issue became problematic?

The fact that he did continue to keep going points to a system that at the very least is not quite so monolithic as it is painted. Tarkovsky plainly had friends as well as enemies; as Eisenstein before him had, and as Dovzhenko had. The battles that Tarkovsky went through, with their odd mixture of luck and contingency, take us back to similar great cinematic battles in the 1930s and 40s. One is faced with the same apparent contradiction: that despite the fiercest overall control of Soviet culture, works of titanic spiritual integrity (Eisenstein's *Ivan the Terrible* being only one of them) continued to emerge. In general, and for reasons that at best remain anecdotal, the actual persecution of film-makers seems to have been far less severe than the contemporary persecution of writers. (Herbert Marshall, in his book *Crippled Creative Biographies*, mentions only two disappearances from the film world, both incidentally of Jewish artists: Eisenstein's tormentor Shumyatsky was shot; and I. Trauberg was swallowed up in the camps.)*

The complex issue of spiritual freedom may be examined a bit more clearly if we glance at two strong but not excessively well known traditional directors, Yuli Raizman (born 1903) and Iosif Heifitz (born 1905), whose careers, starting in the late 1920s, have lasted until the present time. Their films of the 1930s are difficult to specify as either 'conformist' or 'independent'. *The Last Night* (Raizman, 1936) and *The Baltic Deputy* (Heifitz, 1936), for example, both take episodes from the Revolution and treat them according to the standard prescriptions laid down by Socialist

---

*Consider for comparison Ilya Ehrenburg's estimate that of the 700 writers who attended the first Writers' Conference in 1934, a mere 50 survived to the second, twenty years later. Even allowing for natural causes, the attrition rate is astonishing. Svetlana Alliluyeva, Stalin's daughter, adds in her memoirs further corroboration about the traditional immunity of film-makers: 'In those days, before the war, it wasn't the custom for the Party to criticise films and insist that they be remade. They were seen, approved and then released for public distribution. Even if something wasn't quite right nothing happened to the film or those who made it.' (*20 Letters to a Friend*, London, 1967, p. 156.)

Realism: positive heroes, simple contestatory action, speeches, crowds, friendly references to Lenin and the leadership. But in both cases episodes which might seem to us equivocal (for example, the denunciation of 'spies', or the cold-blooded shooting of 'looters') seem to be balanced by other, gentler passages where there is pathos and a wry sense of humour. It is difficult at this late date to make up one's mind about such films. Heifitz and Raizman are both still (1987) alive, and one can meet them. But one of the things one doesn't ask at such interviews – because, eventually, it is impossible to get an answer of sufficient simplicity – is what they truly thought about Stalin and Stalinism.

I have mentioned two films; and there are others from the 30s, not necessarily about Communism at all (for example, *Flyers* by Raizman, 1935; *Hectic Days* by Heifitz, 1935), which confirm the suggestion that one should not be over-censorious. However, by the late 1950s, the 1960s and early 1970s we move into a different sphere of lucidity altogether. Heifitz is famous for exquisite adaptations of Chekhov, such as *The Lady With the Little Dog* (1960) and *In the Town of S* (1966). Here, in wonderfully spacious, 'breathing' film dramas, the vagaries of the human heart are captured with wholly adult seriousness. And oddly, this is equally true for such modern-setting works as *Days of Happiness* (1964), *Married for the First Time* (1979) and *The Accused* (1986). Similarly with Yuli Raizman's later films, two in particular: *Can This Be Love?* (1961), an outstanding study of adolescence, and *A Strange Woman* (1977), a study of divorce. Such films refuse to be condescended to; they remain by any criterion extraordinarily achieved works of world cinema. Now, their greatness can to a certain extent be put down to the artists' own growing maturity; but one feels, unmistakably, that it is also a matter of the times. Even as early as the mid-1950s (when Tarkovsky arrived at film school) absolute monolithic state control had had its day.

Here one might bring in Mikhail Romm who, as Tarkovsky's teacher at VGIK, the Moscow State Film Academy, was in a position to open (or close) cultural horizons. Romm himself made films in the 30s that are, in fact, considerably more bloodthirsty, two of them at any rate, than anything signed by Heifitz and Raizman. The two I am thinking of, *Lenin in October* (1937) and *Lenin in 1918* (1939), are still, apparently, widely shown to Soviet youth. The occasional jarring ruthlessness which forms a passing episode in *The Last Night* or *The Baltic Deputy* becomes, in a film like *Lenin in 1918*, an enveloping miasma of corruption. The film is propaganda for the purges, and a straightforward apologia for terrorism; morally, it is irredeemably bankrupt. Was Romm responsible for this, we ask, or only the servant of orders? Impossible, now, to say clearly. What is important is that by the time we are interested in, the mid-1950s, there is no suggestion that this director was anything but a humane and wise counsellor. Andrei Konchalovsky, Tarkovsky's collaborator and colleague, speaks of Romm's calmness and generosity. 'Calm himself, he loved passionate people.'* Again: 'His gift was the emphasis he placed on the student's spiritual development. He was interested in teaching us not only to become film-makers but to become men.' Again: 'He would listen; and if he was convinced he would say "do it!"' Is it right to speak of salvation here, or was the whole stance one of hypocrisy? One thing (according to Konchalovsky) is certain: 'The 20th Party Congress [February 1956, when Khrushchev denounced Stalin's crimes] was sacred to him. It was his inner guiding light and criterion.'

Stalin's death; the 20th Party Congress; a growing new sense of artistic openness: these are some of the factors surrounding Tarkovsky's emergence – not of course 'explaining' it, but maybe helping it to happen. Is it possible to measure how unique Tarkovsky's achievement was, then, in the context of the general cultural climate I have been describing? The mid-1950s saw a significant increase in film production (from five films in 1952, to 45 in 1954, and 66 in 1955), and with it the drawing into the system of a new pool of much younger talent. These artists, give or take a few years, one might call Tarkovsky's contemporaries. Plainly it is impossible in a short study like this to mention all of them; but two groups, at least, seem important enough to pause over. On the one hand there is the group of directors – Elem Klimov, Larissa Shepitko, Gleb Panfilov, Nikita Mikhalkov, Alexei Guerman, Vasily Shukshin are some of them – who, while dealing with subjects that are in certain ways 'Soviet', push the investigation in directions where freedom of thought becomes an issue. On the other hand, we find a roughly homogeneous group of Southern (Georgian and Armenian) directors – Sergo Paradjanov, Otar Ioseliani, Tengiz Abuladze, Georgy Shengelaya – who become relevant to Tarkovsky's project because of specific cultural and religious affinities.

The first group, being larger and more subtly variegated, is the

*Interview in *Positif*, no. 136, March 1972.

4

harder to talk about. The question of how, and where, a film 'travels beyond the limitations' of 'Soviet' plainly involves, in a way that can't be ducked, the critic's own ideological predisposition as to what is at stake in such distinctions. Is there anything wrong with 'Soviet', some will ask. Others, particularly Russian émigrés in the West, find it impossible that any film showing any aspect of Soviet society in a positive light can ever be truthful or moving. What would this latter category make of films like *I'd Like to Speak* (Gleb Panfilov, 1975), or *Wings* (Larissa Shepitko, 1966)? Both films are portraits of figures of a certain maturity (women in either case) who also occupy a public position in life. Petruchina (Maya Bulgakova) in *Wings* is a high school principal with a distinguished career behind her in the Air Force; Uvarova (Inna Churikova, the director's wife) in *I'd Like to Speak* is first an official, and then mayor, of a provincial Russian city. Both women appear to be happily communist.

The official status of these figures draws the films into areas of public life that we don't on the whole find in Tarkovsky's work. There is an investigative, documentary aspect to them on one level: one sees how Soviet committees work; there are fascinating glimpses of street and home life in their busyness and summertime leisure. Both films are in the broadest sense about civic and moral responsibility. The women feel in their different ways (it is a measure of their never-abandoned socialism) that moral standards have somehow fallen off. If they look back wistfully to the past, they are nevertheless not priggish in their actions; the viewer comes to feel that 'duty' is internalised in their lives as it ought to be – a complex moral category making allowance for other people's weaknesses.

Critics who object to this kind of film (both movies, I ought to say, are meticulously shot and edited) presumably do so on the assumption that any work of art which shows public life in the Soviet Union as 'normal' must be false and hypocritical by definition. Such an *a priori* argument, in either its grandeur or its arrogance, cannot be refuted in a study like this. I am not a Russian myself, and, at bottom, would have to confess that I don't know. So one is forced back on one's experience and intuition. The films do seem to me to be rather extraordinary in the end. Their spiritual dimension is genuine, revolving round the hesitations of the protagonists (about what can and can't be legitimately 'demanded'), their self-doubts, their private gaiety and melancholy: in a word, their thoughtfulness. Though both films are excellently structured, they possess the rarest of all freedoms in a drama, the ability to *seem* contingent (open, dialectical). If they are not 'religious' in any European sense, neither nowadays is most Western art. The weathered stoicism of such films finally moves and convinces the viewer.

These are only two examples of films that are serious, patriotic and personal. One might mention others: *You and I* (1971) and *The Ascent* (1976) by Shepitko for instance, or *Vassa* (1982) and *The Theme* (1978) by Panfilov, along with powerfully intelligent works like *My Friend Ivan Lapshin* (1984) by Alexei Guerman, *Come and See* (1984) by Elem Klimov, *Without Witnesses* (1983) by Mikhalkov and *The Red Snowball Tree* (1974) by Shukshin. But we must move on to the other group of Tarkovsky's contemporaries whom I have labelled (a bit loosely) the Georgians. The Soviet south of course is different from Moscow in being slow, traditional, self-willed. There is a way by which Georgia, despite being Stalin's birthplace, has never really been 'converted' to Marxism. The measure of independence that follows is coupled, in filmic terms, to an admiration for the contingent, the spectacular and the dreamlike – all of which opens avenues to Tarkovsky. Otar Ioseliani, Georgy Shengelaya, Tengiz Abuladze, lastly (perhaps especially) Sergo Paradjanov are the film-makers I am thinking of.

The films of Otar Ioseliani, the first of these directors, are the films of a man who evidently enjoys the pleasures of wine, music, conversation, love. Behind his work is the informing presence of peasant-bourgeois values. A teaching post at the University of Tiflis allows him to treat film-making as itself a semi-artisan activity. Astonishingly, he seems free to work only when he wants to. The personal qualities that have taken him to this enviably independent position – much more independent, after all, than that of many Western film directors – can only be surmised in the absence of immediate first-hand knowledge. One guesses that official Soviet approval meshes, by some complicated mechanism, into a system of traditional, locally based power relations, among which Ioseliani occupies a position somewhat near that of a patriarch. Actually the subject of his films is the clandestine sociability – and extensiveness – of the family in the face of the rules of officialdom. There is, as it were, what officially goes on, and what really goes on. *Pastorale* (1975), his greatest film, gives a glimpse of present-day life in small-town agricultural Georgia: days that are made up of delicate jostlings for position, bargaining for favours and exemptions – everywhere a subtle, pervasive

6

corruption which is not however treated (as it used to be in the Czechoslovakian cinema of the 1960s) as the subject of tolerant comedy, but gravely and obliquely, within a densely textured context of realism. At the heart of the film lies a stabilising innocence: that of an adolescent girl (Nana Ioseliani, the film-maker's daughter) who finds herself looking after the house during the stay of a visiting string quintet. It is a beautiful portrait of the awakening adolescent heart – profoundly penetrating, and at the same time delicate and modest. The film is edited with an impeccable rhythmical freedom, like the work of early Renoir or Vigo. What minimal plot there is slowly dissolves, as if no longer required, in front of the sheer richness of everyday experience. Few enough artists can make us feel life in its savour (the cries of birdsong at twilight, the faraway melancholy of the millstream, the majesty of the moon at midnight shining from behind its envelope of cloud). Gathering these things together in their freshness is the gift of a genuine poet.*

Abuladze and Shengelaya have both had quite long careers, even if neither man's films have been much shown in the West. The two exceptions are interesting. Abuladze's film *The Wishing Tree* (1977) is subtitled *Sketches from Life in Pre-Revolutionary Georgia*; while Shengelaya's *Pirosmani* (1969, not distributed in the United Kingdom till 1980) is a portrait of the city of Tiflis seen through the eyes of its native painter, Niko Pirosmanashvili, at the turn of the century. One senses immediately that the reconstruction is in both cases more than a mere formal exercise in archaeology. The effort of love that goes into each film is governed by patriotic, nostalgic allegiances. Perhaps one can put this most clearly by saying that in neither film is life in pre-Revolutionary Russia 'explained' by reference to post-Revolutionary standards of development (and in other words condescended to, patronised). Each reconstruction lives instead in its own isolated and ultimately mysterious difference from the present. They are extraordinarily beautiful films – Abuladze's ebullient and vigorous, Shengelaya's by contrast wistful, proud and melancholy. How interesting they make Georgia, to the foreigner. Incorporated, since Tolstoy's time, into the greater Russian empire, the republic belongs also to an older and more frankly pagan culture. Everything is odd and

*Other films by Ioseliani are *April* (1961, unreleased), *When Leaves Fall* (1966), *There Was a Singing Blackbird* (1972) and *Favourites of the Moon* (1984, shot in Paris).

7

Shengelaya's *Pirosmani*

'askew'. Each section of the community in Abuladze's film – priest, lawgiver, schoolmaster, peasant – possesses his own interpretation of the world, a huge kaleidoscopic congeries of custom, precept, superstition, poetry and proverb. Putting it thus maybe makes the film sound folkloric; but it is not really the temperature of the experience. Underneath the colourful presence of custom, serious matters of the heart are contemplated. A peasant bride is accused of adultery (in Abuladze's film) and led in a white shift through a crowd of villagers who pelt her with stones until she dies. From her grave a pomegranate tree springs and bursts into blossom. 'Truly, where does beauty come from?' queries the voice-over on which the film concludes: the same question (and asked with the same seriousness) that Ioseliani is asking in *Pastorale*.

In *Pirosmani*, the longed for revelation is unrelated to the beauty of women: the artist, Pirosmani, is asexual. Rather it is the beauty of old stones and crooked street corners. The film is about the taverns and palaces and bourgeois drawing rooms of ancient Tiflis, fantastically reconstructed by Shengelaya by reference to paintings and photographs of the period. There is very little dialogue.

The emphasis instead is on the simple visual splendour of the past. The sensibility of the film is 'aesthetic', but with none of the corresponding effeteness that attaches to that description in the West. *Pirosmani* was made in the same year as Godard's *Weekend* and Bergman's *Shame*; and it is fascinating to contemplate that while Western film-makers in the wake of the student disturbances of 1968 were striking out in gestures of liberal despair, a Georgian film-maker should find *his* artistic identity in an act of conservative homage. Is the true value of the past understood best of all, we might wonder, in those countries where – ostensibly on behalf of the citizens – History has been systematically 'revised'?

The fourth of these Georgian directors, and in fact the most important for our purposes, is Sergo Paradjanov. Paradjanov was born in Tiflis (Tbilisi) of Armenian parents (in 1924, so eight years Tarkovsky's senior). After studying music at the local conservatoire, he moved (1946) to Moscow to enrol at VGIK under Savchenko and Romm. Graduating in 1952, he arrived at Kiev in the Ukraine, working at the Dovzhenko Film Studios, and in 1965 (when *Andrei Roublev* was being shot) filmed a major masterpiece, *Shadows of Our Forgotten Ancestors*, a love tale placed among the mountainous Gutzul tribe on the Carpathian-Ukrainian border. Heralded and applauded abroad (the film won prizes at several international festivals), Paradjanov found himself at home running into the sort of obstruction and mistrust that Tarkovsky would shortly experience with *Andrei Roublev*. Between 1965 and 1968 none of his projects received official backing (they included, apparently, adaptations of Pushkin, Lermontov and H. C. Anderson). In 1968 he moved to ancestral Armenia where under the auspices of Armenfilm he managed to complete a second extraordinary venture, *The Colour of Pomegranates*, an evocation, in cameos, of the life of the legendary 18th-century poet-prince Sayat Nova.

No more than *Shadows of Our Forgotten Ancestors* did this film find sympathy with the authorities, who ordered the veteran film-maker Yutkevich to edit it in Moscow (in the process shearing off 20 minutes) before allowing it to be shown, briefly, in 1973. Meanwhile Paradjanov had fallen into serious personal trouble with the civil powers. In 1973 he was arraigned on charges of illegal currency dealing, homosexuality and 'incitement to suicide'. I know little about his personal life, but enough to guess that this harassment was to a large extent political. (Paradjanov is an outspoken and unrepentant Southern nationalist.) The bogus

9

homosexuality charge was upheld, causing the director to be imprisoned for four and a half years, between April 1974 and December 1978, at which date he was released on an amnesty. But after a further four years of repeatedly blocked projects he found himself arrested again, this time on charges of 'attempting to bribe an official'. Acquitted at a second trial in Tiflis in November 1982, he has completed at the time of writing only one further film, *The Legend of the Suram Fortress* (1985) – like *Pomegranates* a static 'cameo-poem', in several acts or episodes, set this time in ancient Georgia.

Paradjanov, then, like Tarkovsky, faced profound official opposition; which fact alone might be enough to link the two men. But there is more. More perhaps than any of the film-makers mentioned so far, Paradjanov brings into his films a reflection on culture that is free from the dominance of contemporary secular state ideology. The social ideals which his films investigate and stand for are ancient, religion-based, and unrelated to the drama of Communism. The director, it seems, wishes to go back, like Tarkovsky, over the decades, into the last century, to find evidence of relationships that are based not on the ideological appeal to progress, but on local art, piety and nationalism.

Lest his programme sound dauntingly reactionary (the word in this writer's vocabulary is not always a pejorative epithet), I ought briefly to talk about these films' content and imagery. In *Shadows of Our Forgotten Ancestors* – shot, like all three major works, in resplendent colour – the first thing you notice is the beauty of the actors' costumes: extraordinary emblems in fawn, braid and scarlet, further decorated, in the women's case, with prominent bronze and horn jewellery. Hidden in a remote corner of the Tsarist empire there appears to be a rich, variegated peasant society; and what you grasp immediately from the camera's sensuous appropriation of the terrain is that the film-maker doesn't *mind* that this society should be rich, in fact exults in it. As we watch the film we see Paradjanov, as if in an act of repentance, metaphorically casting aside the envy, the rancorous desire for sameness, the mad egalitarianism that led, in the 1930s, to the wiping out of the independent peasant class. The film, a centenary homage, is set in the 1860s; but the inhabitants of the region (who form the body of actors) remain, in essence, authentically the same as they were then. The film shows beautifully a type of life governed first by Christianity, but then by a love of nature, symbolised in the twin imagery of wood (in the lowland region) to

Paradjanov's *The Colour of Pomegranates*

build their shingled houses with, and wool (in the highland pastoral) to provide clothing.

The Carpathians were Paradjanov's by adoption; Armenia, in *The Colour of Pomegranates*, more Eastern, 'classical' and luxurious, is the authentic land of his ancestors. The latter film is an equally extraordinary homage to custom and tradition. Here the mode of life, too, is pastoral, but with an added sensuousness, or perhaps we should say gentleness, that is none the less congruent with the history of a proud, fierce, warrior-producing nation. There is, we are tempted to say, a Christianity of the plough (hardworking, northern, 'Gothic'), and a Christianity of the lamb (passionate, aesthetic, semi-pagan); to which latter category

Armenia, of all nations, attaches traditional poetic allegiance. Fantastic images of wool, therefore, haunt the film – fleeced, carded, combed. And with them another imagery: the great vats of coloured dye in which the fleeces are soaked transpose indifferently at various moments of the film into the red of the pulped vine, the red of the pomegranate, the red finally of the blood of the saints' and warriors' martyrdom. The film's richness is 'liquid' (as it always is in Tarkovsky's films), never more so than in the extraordinary shot of the illuminated bibles and gospels drying out on the church roof, the wind riffling through the pages after a sudden summer downpour.

The Colour of Pomegranates I judge to be a very great film. The musical-religious and the sensuous are authentically combined in it, in a way that one knows of in no comparable work of the West. Paradjanov's next film, *The Legend of the Suram Fortress*, is also extremely beautiful; but it fails to capture the organic quality, the sense in which every scene is an epiphany, which is such a notable feature of the director's earlier work. The debilitating history of Paradjanov's persecutions may speak for itself. Yet the two films, *Colour of Pomegranates* and *Shadows of Our Forgotten Ancestors*, would seem to me almost alone to justify a study of contemporary Soviet cinema. The society that can produce such works of art – linking up as they do with *Andrei Roublev* and *The Mirror* – has reserves of freedom, reserves of energy, that urgently call to us.

Historical note

The attitude of Soviet film-makers towards the pre-Revolutionary past has always had an element (and sometimes very much more than an element) of ambivalence about it. It can be traced in certain ways right from the beginning. For all the relish with which Eisenstein, for example, enjoyed toppling the statue of the Emperor Alexander III in *October* (1928), who can deny that the photographed grandeur of Petrograd, with its palaces, bridges, gateways and monumental caryatids, carries still, in the film, a certain aesthetic authority, inseparable from a proud, aristocratic provenance? Even as he mocked Kerensky in the same film for 'Napoleonism', Eisenstein must have sensed that the grand, the imperial, the regal were also his own destiny aesthetically speaking – to find their flowering in *Alexander Nevsky* and *Ivan the Terrible*.

Nor, probably, is Eisenstein an isolated exception. For all that the authorities wished to eradicate the 'poison' of Western bourgeois influence, they kept coming back to it (during the 1920s at any rate) as iron to a magnet. How they dealt with it and assimilated it is an extremely interesting question. From numerous films in the 20s let us take one in particular, scripted by Lunacharsky, the commissar for culture, called *The Bear's Wedding* (1926). It is an apolitical vampire story set in an imagined Lithuania, in a large brooding castle which Lunacharsky calls, in his programme note, a 'toadstool of corruption'. The audience sits back and confidently awaits the gallery of caricatured despotic noblemen that is bound to follow. But it never happens. Instead, the upper-class characters when they appear are invested with a grave dignity, a realism even – as if the film-makers and actors, despite the fratricidal civil war and the reorganisation of civil society that followed it, had never forgotten, never intended to forget, the gestures, the charm and the amenity of the world they had helped to destroy.

Or we could take a film-maker like Grigori Kozintsev (1905–1973). Kozintsev started his career in the FEKS (Factory of the Eccentric Actor) group in the 1920s: pro-revolutionary, and by definition satirical of the old established imperial institutions. Even, however, as we watch this film-maker grappling with the 'nightmare world' of nineteenth-century St Petersburg in his adaptation of Gogol's *The Cloak* (1926), it comes through to us that this society may possess, in certain regards, a felt, experienced superiority to the present: a greater liveliness anyway, greater humour, malice and variety. The critic can't 'attack' such cultural forms successfully without knowing about them; and the more he knows, the more sophisticated, if not sceptical, he is liable to grow about their 'abolition'. So it was perhaps that Kozintsev in a later phase of artistic creativity became, like Heifitz, one of the great serious adaptors of the classics. David Thomson (in his *Biographical Dictionary of the Cinema*) labels this culminating work academic. But for me, films like *Don Quixote* (1957), *Hamlet* (1964) and *King Lear* (1971) represent a certain kind of artistic perfection. It is not just the immensely grand scale in which they are imagined (though that is always impressive) but something harder to define: their perfect taste, rising out of a flawless knowledge of the different estates of society – popular, bourgeois and aristocratic. Each of which is calmly and gravely celebrated.

Of course, an admiration for the classics has never *not* been part of Soviet ideology. Lenin led the way, with selected permissions.

Mikhail Romm, for instance, was celebrated for knowing *War and Peace* 'by heart'. There must have been in the past, I suppose, numerous standard costume pictures whose orthodoxy and realism don't move us to speculate one way or the other about the deeper allegiance of their makers. Occasionally, however, directors do arise about whom one feels that the past is indeed a passion, and, in the last resort, a criticism of the present. Kozintsev I guess was such a man; Tarkovsky too. No one really knows for certain with directors like Heifitz, Mikhalkov, Gerasimov, Panfilov, for they sensibly keep their private counsel. We look at the works themselves, and make up our own minds, when we are able to.

EARLY YEARS

Andrei Arsenevich Tarkovsky was born on 4 April 1932 in the little village of Zavrozhne, in the Ivanovno region about 60 miles north of Moscow. The Tarkovsky ancestors, it is said, were aristocrats from the Daghestan region in Soviet southern Asia, beyond the Caucasus. Something of Tarkovsky's fierce oriental good looks may be put down to this provenance. We learn that his grandfather was a member of the Narodnaya Volya (People's Freedom) movement which went round preaching culture in the villages. He earned the displeasure of the Tsar and was banished for his liberal views. Tarkovsky's father, the poet Arseny Alexandrovich, was born in the city of Elizavetgrad, now Kirovgrad, in the southern Ukraine in 1907. After the disturbances of the Civil War (in which, while still a boy, he had a number of hair-raising adventures) he found himself accepted in the late 1920s at the Moscow Literary Institute, where in due course he met and married Maja Ivanovna Vishnakova.

The facts of this couple's early life together are alluded to in Tarkovsky's great autobiographical film *The Mirror* (1974). The marriage was not particularly successful. Arseny chose to absent himself, working as a translator since it was impossible to make a living as a poet. The mother, who had originally dreamed of a literary or academic career, was forced to bring up Andrei and his little sister Marina by herself, earning her living as a proof-reader in the First State Printing House in Moscow. One doesn't get the feeling, however, that this was a broken home in the conventional sense. The mother continued to worship her deserting husband all her life; he in turn, as we see from the film, returned home at intervals and took some care in the nurture of his children. Arseny, now recognised as one of Russia's major contemporary poets, was a complicated man, the lover of more than one woman.* Perhaps

---

*Collections of verse include *To Earth, What is of Earth* (poems composed between 1941 and 1966), *Before the Snow* (1941–1962) and *The Harbinger* (1966–1971). As for the spiritual-erotic milieu in which his poetry was conceived, it is interesting that Arseny (who is still alive) is reputed to have been at different times the lover of both Anna Akhmatova and Marina Tsvetayeva.

equally to the point, Andrei's own internal spiritual equilibrium seems not to have been affected by his parents' separation, for he continued to revere both with an intensity and honour attested to by numerous homages in his work.

Was it, incidentally, a Christian household? In the 1920s a number of intellectuals went back to religion (the Jewish writer Nadezhda Mandelstam discusses this phenomenon fascinatingly in the biography of her husband Osip*). It was not so much a clandestine allegiance in the sense of a secret following of observances (like the recusant Catholics in the Reformation), more a matter of general cultural sympathy. In addition, backing up the Tarkovsky Christianity and informing it was the always available presence in the household of the Russian literary classics in handed down editions, along with old-fashioned art albums of painters like Leonardo and Michelangelo. If none of these books was Orthodox Christian in the strict theological sense, they none the less breathed an ethical language informed by classical Christianity. And to be open to their influence provided, during Andrei's childhood, at least the glimpse of an alternative to the official atheist state socialism imparted at school.

Andrei's schooling began in Moscow in 1939, but was interrupted after two years when the war commenced against Hitler, and he returned with his mother to Zavrozhne. (Arseny in the meantime went off as a correspondent for the Red Army newspaper; he lost a leg and was decorated in combat.) School was resumed back in bleak Moscow in 1943. Andrei, it turns out, was merely an averagely gifted pupil. As a child he was a dreamer more than a thinker. More important than the academic work, undoubtedly, was the seven-year musical education which accompanied the official one, supplemented in his last three years at school by drawing classes at the '1905' Academy. He was nurtured, he said later in a filmed interview with Donatella Baglivo, to be an artist. A composer, a painter, a writer: there was never any doubt from earliest times that he would follow one of these metiers.

But the actual route to becoming a film-maker was, as in the nature of things, a little accidental. In 1951 he had enrolled in the School of Oriental Languages to study Arabic; the course wasn't congenial (he spoke later of Arabic being a hard abstract language, like mathematics). A concussion he received on the sports field held up his progress, throwing him back during his second year on

*Hope Against Hope, London 1971.

his own resources. He became interested in geology, and in 1953 joined as an unpaid assistant an expedition arranged by the Kirghiz Gold Institute to explore the minerals of the Turuchansk region, in central northern Siberia. Here he worked for a year, in the process travelling hundreds of miles by himself on foot across the marshy pine forest (or 'taiga') near the Kureyka river. The feeling for living landscape that is such an important part of his identity as an epic film-maker must have been increased by these solitary journeyings.

Back in Moscow in 1954, a year after Stalin's death, Tarkovsky enrolled at VGIK, the Moscow State Film School, where his teacher was the celebrated veteran Mikhail Romm.* The course lasted for six years, taking in all aspects of the cineaste's art: writing, direction, cinematography, sound, decor and acting. We may imagine Tarkovsky at this stage of his life – handsome, quick-eyed, sure of himself, still imbued with the child's sense that 'anything at all is possible if you will it hard enough.' Later on, and with the accretion of fame, Tarkovsky became the most gentle of men, but in his twenties he was a fighter and bohemian. His colleague Andrei Konchalovsky remembers scrapes, including one where Vadim Yusev, the cameraman, got his jaw broken by an accidental 'flyer' of Tarkovsky's when attempting to break up a drinking fight. Fortunately it wasn't taken too personally, and Yusev recovered to become one of the most valuable of Tarkovsky's collaborators – along with Konchalovsky himself (following an independent career), the musician Ovchinnikov and the set decorator Chernyaev. As well as the great Russian directors (whom Romm was teaching), they were all of them fascinated by Western film-makers: Buñuel, Bresson, Bergman. Later, they fell under Kurosawa's and Fellini's influence. Though Tarkovsky has minor complaints about these things in his book *Sculpting in Time*, it appears that everything important in film history could be studied at VGIK. The films of these Western masters, even if not widely shown in the Soviet Union, were available for student emulation.

Tarkovsky completed two films during his stay at VGIK, *There Will Be No Leave Today* (1959) and *The Steamroller and the Violin* (1960), his diploma film. The first of these is really only a mood

*1901–1971. Besides *Lenin in October* and *Lenin in 1918*, Romm's films include *Boule de Suif* (1934), *The Thirteen* (1937), *Nine Days of One Year* (1962), and *Ordinary Fascism* (1965). His last film, *Nonetheless, I Believe* (1971), was completed after his death by Elem Klimov.

piece. Shots display the leader of a scientific expedition waiting on the jetty for a boat which will bring in a bundle of papers, including a vital 'correction' to the expedition's calculations. The weather is stormy: the beams of a lighthouse circle and disappear into the darkness; a lamp on the table picks out the wireless in harsh relief. The atmosphere is one of dense expectation and suspense (no music on the soundtrack). Plainly the work makes reference to Tarkovsky's lonely experience with the Kirghiz Gold Institute expedition (but, interestingly, it is the only moment in Tarkovsky's oeuvre to do so explicitly).

The Steamroller and the Violin is a long-short film: a 46-minute work, made at Mosfilm, in collaboration with a local children's foundation. The story, shot very largely without dialogue, recounts a little boy's friendship with a worker laying tarmac in the boy's home courtyard. The lad (6 or 7 years old) is a timid young musician who had previously had to run the gauntlet of older, bullying children. The asphalt-layer gives the young violinist confidence and, in one scene, the courage to intervene when an even younger child is being bullied. (He restores his football.) Various scenes follow the little boy to his music lesson across the city (where an unsympathetic teacher instils musicianship by the aid of a metronome); these scenes introduce us to a little pig-tailed co-musician, to whom the boy offers an apple (as will happen again in *Ivan's Childhood*); show us an old house being knocked down by a demolition team; and finally take us to the moment when, after a briefly patched up misunderstanding, the boy innocently and fervently plays his violin to the asphalt-layer, demonstrating for the first time (perhaps to the surprise of both of them) the unmediated power of art. It is not quite the end, however, for a later rendezvous between the boy and the asphalt-layer is blocked by the boy's mother, who keeps him locked up in his room. But in a coda, in hindsight recognisably Tarkovskian, he dreams of running towards the steamroller and freedom.

Without being startlingly profound or original (it owes a certain amount, perhaps too much, to the contemporary French short *The Red Balloon* by Albert Lamorisse), the film is successful and well made. The brilliance of Tarkovsky's later work with children is foreshadowed, along with the film-maker's directing belief in the seriousness and responsibility of art. If the film fits in well enough with contemporary Soviet ideology, one is none the less particularly interested in the scene involving the destruction of the ancient house (much of this activity was going on in Moscow at the time). The steamroller itself and its driver are obvious enough 'symbols' of Soviet construction. But some of the quieter regrets harboured in the film's sub-text belong, perhaps, to older, more traditional allegiances.

IVAN'S CHILDHOOD

The Great Patriotic War – the war against Hitler fought between 1941 and 1945 – is more than a mere memory to the average Russian: it is alive in his consciousness in a way that the equivalent fighting in the West has ceased to be among Europeans and Americans. Over 20 million people perished, almost half the entire casualties of the Second World War. As with Napoleon's invasion in 1812, Russia came within an ace of being subjugated. The same, of course, could be said about France in 1914 and Britain in 1940. Why is the memory of invasion still so important to Russians? It has something to do with the fact that as well as being responsible for untold sorrow, the war was also an awakening, a breaking out from the rancorous internal feuding of the 1920s and 30s. Against a common outside enemy the populace found their own souls again. The fact that, after the war, society tragically turned in on itself again only makes the brief moment of freedom (curious that war can mean freedom) more poignant. Thus it is in numerous books and films that continue to celebrate the period, returning to it again and again as if to some inexhaustible well of significance.

Much of the fiercest fighting took place in the Ukraine, the area of Russia east of the Carpathians, between the rivers Dniester and Dnieper. The province afforded Hitler's southern access into Russia, and it was through the Ukraine that his armies were eventually forced back after Stalingrad. The area has a long history of conquest and occupation. Culturally speaking, for example in terms of its church history, it looks westward as much as eastward. In Tolstoy's day and up to the Revolution it was the central wheat-growing province of Russia. Already in the 1930s it had been devastated by one of the worst famines of the century, brought on by the ferocity of collectivisation. Tarkovsky's father is southern Ukrainian by birth (he was born in Kirovgrad, near the river Inga), and the countryside was well known to his son. Here at any event Bogomolov set his novella *Ivan* (written in 1957), adapted for the screen by Tarkovsky (after the cancellation of an earlier effort by E. Abalov) in collaboration with the book's author and Mikhail Papava. Shooting took place at Kaujev on the river Dnieper (with the exception of the idyll in the birch grove everything was shot on location) in the autumn and winter of 1961.

The story involves, in part, seeing the war through the eyes of a child. This would appear to be a traditional artistic procedure in Soviet writing and filming. One finds, for example (in a Soviet encyclopedia), this plot summary of the film *Two Fyodors* made by Marlen Khutsiev four years before *Ivan's Childhood*:

> Two people both named Fyodor meet on a military train – one, a much decorated soldier who has been in the Soviet army in Vienna and Budapest, and the other, a ragged little boy, hunched over a ration tin of gruel. War has directly affected both of them. The elder Fyodor has lost his family and home. The younger Fyodor has lost his parents and has experienced the occupation and hunger. They both need friendship. The elder Fyodor makes his decision unexpectedly, but in fact it is the only possible decision for him. He runs along the station platform after his namesake. Then the two people return to the elder Fyodor's war-devastated home. The soldier has known friendship and its worth in the army; he is softer and kinder than the child, who is often cruel, practical and hard-headed in a very unchildish way, as war has made him.

Here in embryo is the relationship between the generations Tarkovsky sketches in *Ivan's Childhood*. One notes the boy's cruelty and haughtiness. Twenty-five years later, and forty years after the war, the theme has not yet been played out. A recent study of children at war by Elem Klimov, *Come and See* (1984), has been shown to acclaim. The periodic devastations of Russia in the 20th century, not just in the last but also in the previous wars, gave birth to a new social category of *bezprizorniye*, or waifs: there must have been literally thousands of such boys and girls, thousands of such buried stories. Lara's daughter, Katya, in *Doctor Zhivago*, to give a well known example, becomes one of these restless war orphans after being abandoned by her mother in Siberia. She rises to an unprecedented position of influence in the army, achieving 'legendary' status in the manner of Bogomolov and Tarkovsky's Ivan.

Of course, one cannot tell from a mere plot summary whether the working out of a film like Khutsiev's is noble and tender, or whether it falls into 'Soviet' cliché. War films provide as much opportunity for ideological simplification as any other genre, in the sense that an identifiable allegorical opponent, Fascism, is there if the director wants it as a stalking horse, an excuse to think crudely or to lapse into posture and rhetoric. Tarkovsky's film is free from such devices. It neither celebrates victory, nor (in the manner of John Ford) glories in elegiac defeat. The context of the film is war; but the experiences it makes sense of are universal.

The first thing to say is that the characters in *Ivan's Childhood* strike one as being indefinably right: finely imagined, that is to say, and placed in a profound relationship to each other. At the centre of the story are Captain Kholin (Valentin Zubkov), his lieutenant Galtsev (E. Zharikov), and a boy, Ivan (Nikolai Burlyaev, a Moscow schoolboy, later to play the bell-maker in *Andrei Roublev*). As the main body of the film opens (I shall talk about the prologue in a moment) the boy has returned by a river crossing from a successful sortie behind enemy lines bearing important information. Despite his years, he evinces from the moment one sets eyes on him a strange and irrefutable authority: his movements are more like those of a prince or an aristocrat than those of an ordinary boy. Summoning the captain, he discloses his intelligence. But what to do with him now? Are there more missions he can be sent on? Should he be sent on them, seeing that he is so young and vulnerable? Ought he not be sent back to military academy? The film traces the special bond which grows up between the two adults and the child during these deliberations. A paternal bond, of course; but somewhat modified, in that there is already such a relationship between the captain (a handsome, strong, not particularly 'educated' man) and the lieutenant, about eight years his junior.

The delicate growth of these feelings of responsibility of the men towards the boy forms the moral centre of the film. The captain has never married. The child represents in his mind the son he hasn't had. Uncultivated himself, he would like Ivan to have the opportunities for general culture that never came his way. At the same time he is shy of adopting the boy, as the lieutenant quietly urges, feeling in his heart firstly that he is a bit of a 'lout' (as the gruff Lt. Col. Grazhnev calls him), secondly that such an adoption can only hold the child back after the war. He is a soldier, and the skills of a soldier may by then be redundant. The working out of these positions, and why one is forced to be slightly vague about them, is not so much explicit as a matter, across the film, of hints

Responsibilities: Ivan, the captain and the lieutenant in *Ivan's Childhood*

and guesses; we pick them up from the story's progress, rather than having them explained. One of the striking things about the film is the tender realism with which it approaches this question of 'life chances'. The Soviet ideology preaches equality of opportunity, but education is intrinsically 'elitist', distinguishing for good or ill the people who are lucky enough to have it from those who are unlucky enough not to. The captain desires it for the child, yet inevitably it will take the child away from him. In *Ivan's Childhood* there is no hypocrisy on this matter. Tarkovsky charts, in the captain's wishes, traditional aspirations about bettering oneself that on the face of it have little to do with communism. And we feel as we watch the film that these wishes come from the man's whole personality; that is to say, from the internal demands of the story, rather than being imposed from outside.

I speak of the relationship between the two men and the boy as a relationship governed by delicacy. This is observable in the facial features as well as in the pauses and glances which Tarkovsky elicits from the interaction of the trio. (There is also a fourth character, a grizzled sergeant, Katasonov, who is later killed.) The face of the captain is handsome and thoughtful, while the features of the boy (aged about twelve) are girlish and refined; those of the lieutenant, though older, are scarcely less so. In a crucial sense the latter has not yet come into manhood. A curious quasi-sexuality exists in the encounters and partings of the three principals (the boy's pouting sulkiness towards the lieutenant, his physical delight in the captain's robust strength). This can be said safely just because of the aforementioned delicacy: the relationship is plainly not 'homoerotic'. Actually the presence of the counterpart feminine is crucial in *Ivan's Childhood*, as it is in all of Tarkovsky's cinema, and perhaps we should speak about it briefly.

Womanhood and girlhood appear in this war film in three complementary guises. First there is Ivan's mother (Irina Tarkovskaya, the director's first wife), whom we briefly see in flashback in the beautiful sequence that opens the film, when Ivan runs to tell her of the cuckoo song. The crane shot seems to lift him right off the ground into the boughs of the trees, before depositing him again on the earth and letting him run to her. She is present, too, in Ivan's extraordinary dream that seems to take place simultaneously at the bottom and the top of a well. At first Ivan is alone at the foot of the shaft. Then mother and son are sitting together looking down the tunnel at the moonbeam shining on the surface of the water. Ivan tries to grasp the silver nugget, but it vanishes as his hand breaks the surface. It is the star of fate, the boy's destiny, which the film will elucidate. Seconds later he is again at the foot of the well, separated from his mother. In a premonition of his death (by guillotine) the bucket falls on him, breaking the vision, or turning it into a nightmare. (At the top of the well another bucket splashes his mother's body, telling us from the posture she is lying in that she too will become a victim of the Germans.) The two brief sequences are extraordinary, both for the power and for the economy with which they distil the emotion of filial longing. Looking forward to *Solaris* and more particularly to *The Mirror*, one sees that this is a constant theme in Tarkovsky's work, present (for all the necessary guilt and anguish that accompany such things in real life) with a beautiful simplicity – an ethical conviction of its importance in the human economy.

The two other feminine presences in the film belong to Ivan's little playmate (Vera Miturich), glimpsed once more, like the mother, in a pair of complementary dreamscapes or memories; and secondly to a pretty doctor, Masha (Valentina Malyavina), who is flirted with at different times by the lieutenant and the captain. The sequences with the child are beguiling: she is present, as we shall see, in the very last shot of the film, but before this there is a sequence where – either a memory or a dream – Ivan and she are travelling along a country road in the back of a lorry full of apples. It is raining. Behind them the sky flashes by, but in 'negative', so that the air is black and the trees seem to be covered in blossom. Ivan offers the little girl three different apples, the last of which she bites into juicily (as the Old Man bites into a similar apple in the famous scene of life and death in Dovzhenko's *Earth*). Three times in this scene we see the little girl's face, each time more grave and sombre. Then the camera is at ground level, the truck pulling away, spilling the apples on to the sand. Horses appear from the side of the road and graze quietly among the unexpected pasture. Why is this scene so touching? Perhaps because it, too, contains Ivan's fate (in the girl's gravity). The boy's delight in his companion's loveliness is his awakening to the existence of the ideal, appropriately marked by the offering to her of a gift. The moment when this awakening happens (if it ever does happen) is a precious moment of childhood experience, beautifully captured by Tarkovsky.

The sequences involving the doctor, just graduated and very young, are also a strong and necessary part of the film. The deliberations between captain and lieutenant about Ivan's adoption make one think of the sort of post-war household that a boy could be taken into, and thus the need, on the part of whoever is doing the adopting, for a wife, or at least a nurturing feminine presence. However, to say that Masha stands for anything so definite as a possible mother-figure is to make the episode unjustifiably allegorical. On the contrary, the scene in which she appears has the sort of gratuitous unexpectedness – the possibility of going 'either way' – that one associates with such adventures. When we first come across her the lieutenant is already partly in love with her but worried about her safety, suggesting that if possible she leave the battle zone. The captain appears at this moment and leads her off, under the lieutenant's gaze so to speak, towards a nearby birch grove, where they walk and converse. The talk is about fear and safety. The captain playfully challenges her to walk along the limb of a fallen tree, which she does, and then refuses his help to come down. Seconds later, however, as she is crossing a ditch, he clasps her in his arms and kisses her. Masha runs away, but comes back to him tenderly placing her head against his shoulders. In his mysterious, inexplicit way the captain woos and wins her.

As well as being fine in itself, the scene may be said to dramatise, rather well, the bitter unfairness of love. The lieutenant is the more suitable consort; but the captain is older and braver. He exists, as the lieutenant does not, at margins of danger which bring a reciprocal reward. The cinema which explores this moral theme well (youth's necessary deference to age) is rare.* The episode seems to unfold in terms of its own internal logic and gesture rather than by the dictates of dialogue.

Right at the end of the film, the girl reappears in the dugout where the captain and the lieutenant are resting after their return from the enemy lines. By now the lieutenant has confirmed her departure and she has come to say goodbye. The gramophone needle slips on the record which the men are playing (it is Chaliapin singing); by the time Kholin has fixed it, the girl has disappeared. She and the captain won't ever meet again, for Kholin, we are told in voice-over, is killed on the way to Berlin. Of such encounters, and lost opportunities, is war fabricated.

Ivan's Childhood, we don't need to be reminded, is a war film. From the cinema's origins – from, say, *Birth of a Nation* and *Intolerance* – it has excelled at giving us the experience of warfare directly. In particular, the peculiar fear of the moments before going into battle. There are one or two such brilliant prior-to-battle sequences in *Ivan's Childhood*: sequences that affect you as much by their closeness to dream as by their uncanny detailed realism (such realism as can never be evoked in the theatre).

One such episode – the central action sequence of the film – is the crossing of the river by the two men and the boy. Ivan, after much argument, is to be despatched again behind enemy lines; but as well as this they are going to rescue the bodies of the executed Russian scouts which have been tied up and left on the opposite bank. The water is still and calm, lit up every few moments by hallucinatory flares. In a silence of concentration the party reaches the opposite shoreline, a marshy undergrowth sprinkled with pale birchwood and clumps of grasses, through which Ivan guides the men up to their knees in water. In the background a tree cracks and falls. A fatality hangs in the air; Ivan in fact will never be seen alive

---

*The only comparable work I can think of is the Polish film *Camouflage* (1978), by Krzysztof Zanussi. Here again we find an episode in which a witty older man, a professor, wins out in love over his handsome young male research student. The conversation on which the plot hinges is dark, sinuous and bitter, ending in blows.

Dream/realism: crossing the river

again. His leave-taking from the two men is filmed with tenderness
(he shakes the lieutenant's hand, embraces the captain). Seconds
later they are separated by a passing German patrol. The captain
and the lieutenant untie the corpses and stow them seated upright
in the canoe between them. During the return crossing, without
Ivan, snow begins to fall on the river.

   This gentle fall of snow, so right at that particular moment, has
the indefinable quality of a musical cadence: to analyse it is to risk
making it evaporate. Though Tarkovsky is capable of planning
such effects, it is interesting that the snow here was apparently
accidental. Yet, strangely, when one has noticed this, one notices
that it ties up with another 'snowstorm' later in the film as the
advancing Soviet troops enter the ruins of Berlin. This time it is
not real snow which falls from the sky, in the cleverly cut
documentary footage, but a whirlwind of white paper documents
issuing from the record chamber of the bombed German Chan-
cery. Among the swirling documents, identifiable from his scowl-
ing photograph, is the death certificate of the captured Ivan. Not

on the conscious level, but on the unconscious, we recognise that the two sequences rhyme. Tarkovsky's films, when they are working well, possess an astonishing tension between the controlled and the unforeseen. Everything seems to be planned and yet at the same time 'open'. His correspondences of editing constitute the reward that comes to an eye which is fanatically unlazy. It is as if Tarkovsky were one of those directors who had only to lay his glance· on the world to confer on it beauty and significance.

The mention of correspondences, with their literary, Baudelairean echo, might seem to be obscure, and I ought to say more clearly what I mean by them. A film exists first of all as a scenario: a great part of the effort of movie-making goes into the basic task of formulating coherent narrative from the written instructions of the shooting-script. Most directors, I think, are content if they even succeed in doing this (since by itself it is so difficult). In first-rate film-makers, however, a refining process is going on simultaneously, best described as a continuous internal mental shaping. It is a surplus of energy and independence, when the project is going well, which enables a film-maker to find what he has to say *visually* rather than narratively. A thousand thoughts are suggested by the correct image or transition which it would take pages of script to unburden. A living film exists, we might say, in such economies of form, such economies as I have been calling 'correspondences', hard as they are to define. *Ivan's Childhood* is full of mysterious poetic assonances which seemingly come out of nowhere and can scarcely have been foreseen in the planning stage.

I use the word 'poetic' with caution: the assonances (internal rhymes) are indeed poetic, emotionally speaking, but translated out into meaning they can be grim and terrible. A series of editing decisions, for example, seems to point explicitly enough to the method of Ivan's execution (almost as if there were a pun on the notions of 'axing' and 'editing'). Towards the end of the film Galtsev discovers, by accident, the boy's death document in the ruins of Berlin. The camera now moves into the death chambers themselves. With documentary austerity the gaze fastens on the hooks attached to the ceiling, before moving over unsteadily to the equally horrible sight of a bloodstained guillotine. A sort of vertigo, or nausea, grips the invisible onlooker, causing the camera to tilt into a spin. When it steadies itself, the head and shoulders of Ivan are to be seen hanging upside down from the top of the frame.

Now the scene changes; it is a summer's day earlier in Ivan's boyhood, on the beach. Ivan is kneeling on the sand in front of a bucket full of water, which he drinks from. The camera is situated from his mother's viewpoint and looks down on to Ivan's naked shoulders and neck. This three-dimensional sculpture of the head (or 'bust' in the Roman sense) has always been one of Tarkovsky's fascinations. In *Stalker*, for example, whole minutes are spent in close-up regard of Alexander Kaidanovsky's features (the sequence of the railway trolley carrying the travellers into the Zone). In the post-credits sequence of *The Mirror*, the camera moves round from in front of Margarita Terekhova's face to study her body from behind as she is sitting on the gate with her hair up. In *Ivan's Childhood*, in the opening sequence, the camera is fixed motionless on the boy's profile (cutting him off at the shoulders), as later, when he is counting out the pods and catkins which itemise the enemy deployment, it sweeps up on to his shoulders from behind. In *Solaris*, finally, there is an extraordinary sequence where, with unconscionable slowness, the image moves in to concentrate on Donatas Banionis' earlobe (more accurately, the hairs that are growing from it).

Ivan makes his report

What these strange epiphanic sequences seem to have in common, despite differences of emphasis, is an absolutely intense regard for the vulnerability – I am tempted to say the sacredness – of the human form. We have to be careful in describing it, because although such scenes are linked to the body, they are not in fact 'sexual' or erotic; the desire to touch, or even to kiss, which they provoke is essentially protective, unlibidinous. Where other directors (Antonioni, Bergman, Godard perhaps) are tirelessly drawn towards new ways of photographing the male and the female nude, either in gestures of love-making or in repose (this being, in a way, their contribution to art, or, as we should say, their contribution to painting), so the embraces that attract Tarkovsky – focused not on the face but on the earlobes and on the nape of the neck – are governed by a familial tenderness.

The 'skinniness' of Ivan in this last beach scene recalls, in fact, a slightly earlier image in the film, from the interpolated Russian newsreel which introduces the scenes in Berlin. In one shot the six dead children of Goebbels, extracted from the Bunker, are lying dead beside their parents. In a contiguous scene two naked dead children, bullet holes visible in their bodies, are lying on the floor, while their father, a Luftwaffe officer (as we see from his uniform) has hanged himself from a beam in the attic. The images are terrible and pitiable, all the more so in that they belong to photographed fact rather than to staged drama. The serious patriotism which fuels Tarkovsky's vision touches, at moments like this, another emotion, which we might describe as a noble pity, a regard for the conquered, a conviction that in war the innocent suffer along with the guilty.

I am not able to speculate to what extent it was dangerous for Tarkovsky to entertain thoughts like these in 1961, in view of the undying hatred that the Russians harbour towards Nazism. Perhaps there is a humanism in official Soviet ideology which accommodates, or partially accommodates, such reconciliations. But what one feels is that, official ideology or no, these are Tarkovsky's own thoughts on the matter. Midway through the film there is a sequence where Ivan leafs through the pages of an album of Dürer, lent to him by the lieutenant. Pausing before a woodcut of 'The Knight, Death and the Devil', the child says – speaking of the figure of Death – that he once saw a German like that, on a motorbike. There might be a way in which the placing of such a comment would be didactic, oversignalled, sententiously designed to make a point (that the Germans are monsters). But it is more complicated than this, for it is plain that the prints themselves are very beautiful. Galtsev doesn't answer Ivan, instead looks thoughtful. The Book (in this case the album of drawings) has a private, quasi-sacred status as art, utopianly crossing the boundaries of Nation. (Characteristically, the scene is one of the additions Tarkovsky made to the original story by Bogomolov in order to deepen its historical resonance.)*

It is this singular independence of spirit which even at this early stage gives Tarkovsky's work the edge over other contemporary Soviet film-makers. All the more striking that this attribute should be evident in a first film, made in the director's late twenties. Tarkovsky arrived on the scene – as the Venice film festival recognised in awarding *Ivan's Childhood* the Golden Lion (shared with the Italian film-maker Zurlini) – almost with the *éclat* of the young Orson Welles. We note that the marks of his mature style are already firmly present, down to, and especially, the private vocabulary of fire and water: fire (the softly burning logs in the dug-out's stove) as well as water, the river landscape and the steady drip of the tap that 'sets off' the dream of the well-shaft.

Might it be interesting, then, in this context, to compare *Ivan's Childhood* with a somewhat contemporary Soviet work like *The Cranes are Flying* (1957)? Kalatozov's film is in many ways remarkable; it seems to breathe the air of freedom that everywhere affected artistic circles in the Soviet Union in the wake of the 20th Party Congress. Yet there is still, at the edges, something just a little 'official' about it: it is not quite a work of spiritual freedom. The actress, Samoilova, is charming, but the passages that are touching in the film (such as the boy's parting gift to the heroine of

*Tarkovsky fought Bogomolov hard for his changes. In general Tarkovsky supplies throughout a Christian symbolism that is not present in the original – making the dug-out, for example, where Kholin holds his meetings, the husk of a bombed-out Orthodox church (a holy icon is visible in the bombing scene). The director makes sure, too, that the music the men play on their gramophone is sacred Russian chanting (a detail not present in the original). In addition, two symbols of the Cross are worth commenting on. In the first, a fierce bombardment has been sustained in the Soviet trenches. At the end of it the camera comes to rest for a full six seconds on a tilted iron crucifix with the sun setting behind it, image of strength and perseverance. Harder to make out (whether accidental or deliberate) is the glimpse of the crashed Messerschmidt in the river, tilted like the church crucifix, with Luftwaffe Maltese-cross marks prominent on its fuselage. May we surmise, at any event, that the contest, for Tarkovsky, is not solely between Fascism and Socialism, but a contest about evil at the very heart of Christendom?

31

a squirrel) are also sentimental and 'convenient'. More than this: running through the film is a curious unTarkovskian suspicion of art and culture, exemplified by the figure of the seducer, a concert pianist who rapes the heroine while absenting himself from the battle front. The values of the film, in short, when they move away from the delicate Samoilova, are predictably 'sturdy' and socialist. And much the same thing could be said about the other great contemporaneous study of wartime faithfulness, Chukhrai's *Ballad of a Soldier* (1959).

It may sound rather as if I am hostile to these films, which I am not. Their great skill, the 'air of freedom' they breathe, is their lyrical photography. It is surely not merely coincidental that this is equally the beauty of *Ivan's Childhood*. One feels very clearly that Yusev, Tarkovsky's cameraman, is indebted to the example of Urusevsky, the veteran cameraman of *The Cranes are Flying*. There are many fine examples of mobile camerawork in this latter film; but there is no single sequence so intense or so extraordinary as the opening and closing shots of *Ivan's Childhood*. I have already referred to the opening sequences, but the closing shots are equally remarkable. Ivan chases the little girl in a long run over the sands into the shallow sea. Years before the Steadicam, Tarkovsky's horizontal crane extends itself with breathtaking panache and fluency across the water. Compared to this, the shot of the flying cranes which closes Kalatozov's film is 'merely' lyrical or modest.

ANDREI ROUBLEV

In his book *Sculpting in Time*, Tarkovsky speaks of the completion of *Ivan's Childhood* as a watershed. Now there was one feature film behind him, to prove that he really was a film-maker. Psychologically the moment was marked by a huge surge of confidence and ambition. It is in his second film that a film-maker discovers whether his original talent is combined with other equally important qualities, moral as well as aesthetic: whether he has depth and range and staying power. In the event *Andrei Roublev* represents film-making about as physically ambitious as it is possible to contemplate. The daring of the conception (the conjuring up of another historical epoch) is matched by the success of the execution. Yet on the whole, perhaps, one ought not to be surprised by the age at which maturity manifests itself. Tarkovsky was 32 when he began shooting *Andrei Roublev*. Pushkin at the same age had completed *Eugene Onegin*.

The idea of transforming the life of the late medieval monk and icon painter Andrei Roublev into a film was originally that of the actor Vassily Livanov, who in turn had been stimulated by the exhibition celebrating the sixth centenary of the artist's birth mounted by the Soviet authorities in 1960. (As a matter of fact most modern scholars have placed the birth in 1370, not 1360.) Starting in late 1961, as their second collaboration together, Konchalovsky and Tarkovsky continued to work on the screenplay after the year-long interruption of *Ivan's Childhood*. A production contract was signed in 1962. The 'literary scenario' was accepted in December 1963. In April 1964 the authorities gave the film the go-ahead. It was shot between September 1964 and November 1965. (Meanwhile Konchalovsky was working on his own films, *My First Teacher*, 1965, and *Happiness of Asya*, 1966.)

By the time the film was ready for viewing (August 1966), however, the liberalisation that marked cultural affairs in the Soviet Union after the 20th Party Congress seems to have been slowing down. The invasion of Czechoslovakia was still two years off, but already the pockets of freedom were beginning to be sealed. The Soviets discovered one day that they had a 'dangerous'

33

film on their hands. Cuts were demanded, particularly in the scenes showing nudity (episode III) and violence (the raid on Vladimir). Tarkovsky, with characteristic obstinacy, refused. His contract, like all Soviet film contracts, stipulated that excisions could only be made with the permission of the director. Eventually he did allow about 14 minutes to be taken out and later stated that the present version (3 hours 6 minutes) was in fact the one he was happy with. This is the version that was shown among the unofficial entries at Cannes in 1969, receiving the International Critics' Prize. Overall, however, there were enormous delays and frustrations. The film was not so much banned as 'held back from release', finally surfacing in Russian cinemas in October 1971. (After the very wide success of *My First Teacher*, Konchalovsky had similar problems with *Happiness of Asya*.)

The facts about the icon painter Roublev are as fragmentary as those of the life of any Russian artist from a distant epoch. We have already seen that there is an uncertainty about the date of birth. What does seem clear is that by the 1390s he was installed as a monk in the monastery of Troitse-Sergeyeva (Holy Trinity monastery) in Zagorsk, north-east of Moscow. The monastery was ruled at the time by Sergius of Radonezh, later to be revered as one of the greatest of Russian saints. Sergius was a political as well as a religious figure: spiritual adviser to the Muscovite Grand Duke, Dmitri Donskoi. And it seems likely that the first serious commissions Roublev undertook were in the service of Dmitri's quarrelling sons Vassily and Yuri. Yuri (a villain in the film) was territorially based in Zvenigorod, where, in addition to any work he might have done for the prince in a private capacity, Roublev helped decorate the cathedral of the Dormition in the late 1390s.*

By 1400, Roublev had become a monk in the Andronikov monastery in Moscow (now the Roublev museum). 1405, the next important date, finds him in the company of the Byzantine painter Theophanes the Greek decorating the Cathedral of the Annunciation in Moscow. In 1408 he was called to Vladimir to decorate another Cathedral of the Dormition. (Episode V in the film has

---

*In 1919 the youthful Dziga Vertov filmed the opening of Saint Sergius' coffin. Atheists and Christians were poised in ideological conflict, the faithful confidently expecting the body to be preserved uncorrupted. When it was discovered that the tomb contained merely bones and fragments of cloth, Lenin had the newsreel widely distributed for propaganda purposes.

Andrei Roublev with the icon of the Miracle of the Triumphant St George

scenes of the sacking of Vladimir by the Tartars.) For the rest of his fairly long life – he died in 1430 – Roublev remained based in the Andronikov monastery, returning briefly to Troitse-Sergeyeva either in 1411 or at some period early in the 1420s to paint his most famous icon of all, the allegorical picture of the Trinity, in memory of his old patron St Sergius.

The extant work of Roublev is not numerous. His fame rests mainly on the fragments of fresco painting in the Cathedral at Vladimir; the icon of the Holy Trinity just mentioned; and a fine icon of Christ in Glory, painted in Zvenigorod around 1410. Those who have seen these works speak of their extraordinary harmony and beauty. The colours are shimmering and opalescent: pinks, lapis lazulis, pale golds. The human forms are rounded but not soft; the facial expressions of the saints and holy figures are at once austere and compassionate. Roublev's art-historical importance seems to have been in the establishing of a particularly Russian mode of holy representation, breaking away from predominantly

Greek influence (represented in the film by the angular severities of Theophanes). This grave humanism was continued in the following century by the next great Russian painter, Dionysy of Theraponte. But so wide was Roublev's fame that a Church council in 1551 proclaimed his style as the true standard of artistic orthodoxy, 'to be followed in all perpetuity'.*

In order to contextualise the film a little further, a more general word or two about the historical times in which Roublev lived may not come amiss. His lifetime coincided with the first stirrings of Russian reunification, completed in the reigns of Ivan III (1462–1505) and of Ivan IV (The Terrible) (1533–84). The early Christian Russian principality had been based in Kiev (modern Ukraine), moving thence, as the city declined in the 11th and 12th centuries, to Vladimir-Susdal, north-east of Moscow, and to Novgorod, in the north-west corner of Russia, under Sweden. In 1223, meanwhile, had come the shock of the invasion of the Tartars, set in motion in the Mongolian east by the territorial ambitions of the great Genghis Khan. For the next 170 years the principal cities of Russia, with the exception of remote Novgorod, had all been subjected to the Tartar yoke.

In the late 14th century this began to relax. It was the same Dmitri Donskoi, patron of Sergius and father of Vassily and Yuri, who made the first dent in Tartar domination when he defeated the armies of the Golden Horde at the famous pitched battle of Kulikivo (1370). (Tarkovsky had intended to open his film with scenes from this battle, but they were judged too expensive.) Although the Tartars remained in Russia as a formidable presence for another 200 years – one finds them laying siege to Moscow as late as 1571 – their hegemony was decisively broken. In the period in which *Andrei Roublev* is set they were under pressure both from the Muscovites themselves and from the rival conquests of Tamburlaine in the south.

*What knowledge there is of Andrei Roublev in the West owes much to the pioneering scholarship of the traveller and aesthete Robert Byron. Two quotations from his book *First Russia, Then Tibet* (Macmillan, 1933) give the flavour of his enthusiasm. The icon of the Holy Trinity he calls 'the greatest masterpiece ever produced by a Slav painter, a work of unprecedented invention, to which nothing in art ... offered a parallel.' And again, of the same work: 'It was not until the literature of the 19th century that the Slav genius again scaled the heights discovered by an obscure monk, whose one memorial [a slight exaggeration!] is a panel of three angels.' It should be added, I think, that if the gravity of Andrei Roublev's art is entirely his own, its 'sweetness' and spiritual calm have occasionally had him compared to the Italian painter Fra Angelico.

The period is therefore ambiguous. On the one hand we may surmise that it was as full of violence and uncertainty as any comparable period in the Middle Ages (and that violence is shown in full in the film). On the other hand, from an educated Russian's point of view, the time represents also the beginnings of national resurgence. Roublev's paintings can be seen as the cultural symbol of this renaissance. In Tarkovsky's project there were, as it were, opportunities for both optimism and pessimism.

Andrei Roublev, considerably altered from its original conception, is structured in the shape of seven separate imagined episodes describing different stages in Roublev's career. Since it is long and complicated I shall risk giving a fairly extensive synopsis. A dramatic short prologue – in which Andrei himself makes no appearance – shows, first, a man paddling frantically towards us across a river in a coracle. Beaching the craft, he disappears up the tower of a church, emerging breathless to untie the harness of a primitive air balloon, patched together out of skins and parchment. (At the foot of the tower a crowd of monks and peasants inveigh against the godless machine and its pilot.) Undaunted, the inventor clambers on to the skins and casts himself off. The machine sails off over the river, on whose surface far below boats can be seen floating like little models. Quickly the balloon loses height, coming to rest in a tangle of mud and skins on the opposite river bank. A shifting of limbs under the sacking indicates that the pilot is still living (whether harmed or unscathed is not shown).

We now move into the first episode. The year is 1400. Roublev (Anatoly Solonitsin) with his travelling companions Daniel the Black and Kyril take refuge from the rain in a hut. Inside, a jester leaps around singing bawdy songs and performing acrobatics in front of a group of peasants. Suddenly some soldiers appear and arrest the jester. They take him outside and smash his head against a tree, before carrying him away with them. (Oblivious to these happenings, two drunken peasants, one armed with an enormous pole, slither around in the mud fighting each other.)

The next episode (1405) opens in the interior of a church with a conversation between the painter Theophanes the Greek (Nikolai Sergeyev) and one of the monks, Kyril (Ivan Lapikov), whom Theophanes at first mistakes for Andrei. Theophanes wants Andrei to paint with him. Kyril says he will have to ask him himself. Outside, on the great square, prisoners are being tortured on the wheel. Back in the Andronikov monastery Andrei, when

'The Passion of Andrei': Roublev and the pagan gir

approached, meekly accepts his mission; he makes a tearful farewell from the other monk, Daniel (Nikolai Grinko). Now Kyril's barely suppressed jealousy erupts: he abandons the monastery, cursing it for a temple of money-lenders.

Episode III is dated 1406 and entitled 'The Passion of Andrei'. In a woodland glade we first see Andrei scolding his apprentice Foma (he gets him to smear his face with mud). Theophanes appears as if in a vision, seated on a tree trunk, his legs crawling with ants. An elliptical conversation ensues with Theophanes (or his ghost) about the relations of the Russians to the Tartar invaders. This in turn moves into a vision of Calvary in a Russian, snow-bound setting (Christ dragging his cross looks very like Andrei). A Russian Magdalene throws herself at Christ's feet before the setting up of the cross and the driving in of the nails.

Back in the world of reality, we see a party of travellers, including Andrei and Daniel, paddling their boats in the river.

Mists, flares, groves of birchwood. Pagan revellers are scurrying along the banks carrying torches. Having landed, Andrei is spotted, accused of spying, and tied up to a post with threats of crucifixion. Later a beautiful naked pagan girl kisses him on the lips before freeing him. Next morning, at daybreak, as the monks continue their journey by boat, they witness soldiers rounding up the revellers. The girl who had untied Andrei makes a dash for freedom, diving under the boat and swimming out towards the opposite shore.

The fourth episode (Last Judgment, 1408) starts sombrely. The scaffolding is up in the interior of the cathedral in Vladimir, but for some reason Andrei delays commencing the decoration. Outside, near a field in early harvest he converses with Daniel, who cites the bishop's urgency: the delay has been going on for two months and Andrei risks angering the Grand Duke Vassily. A flashback now takes us to an earlier episode involving the building (or decorating) of a palace for this same potentate. There are blinding white walls: dandelion fluff floats in the air. Andrei, visiting the Grand Duke, holds the duke's pretty child in his arms. The party of artisans just finishing the masonry tell the high-ranking official Stepan that they are now off to start a similar palace in Zvenigorod, for the duke's younger brother Yuri. Stepan takes it upon himself to interpret the duke's jealousy. He follows them with a posse, and in an ambush in a wood blinds them with daggers. The memory of this depravity is what is evidently haunting Andrei. Returning to the church, he hurls paint against its pristine walls. An innocent simpleton (Irina Tarkovskaya) comes in to take refuge from the rain. Andrei orders the scriptures to be read. It seems as if (somehow) the spell has been broken.

The next episode, dated autumn 1408, shows a raid on the city of Vladimir. The Grand Duke's brother Yuri has conspired with a Tartar chieftain to seize the city in his brother's temporary absence. (A previous ceremony of reconciliation between the pair, blessed by the Metropolitan, is seen in flashback during this episode.) Andrei himself is present in the cathedral while the sacking takes place and manages to save the simpleton from rape by slaying her abductor with an axe. Cameos from the sacking: 1. Yuri on the roof of the cathedral; behind him in slow motion the victorious Tartars despoil the church of its lead and gilding; 2. Deaths of Foma (shot into a stream) and of another apprentice Sergei, blood spurting from his neck as a two-handled saw vibrates beside him; 3. Interior of the cathedral: having refused to tell the raiders where the treasure is, the sacristan is wrapped in pitch bandages and has boiling oil poured into his mouth. His body is attached to a horse's harness and dragged feet first out of the church; 4. The magnificently mounted Tartar chief, in front of an icon, mocks the Christians for their belief in the Virgin Birth.

In the aftermath of the sacking the ghost of Theophanes again appears in the burnt-out cathedral. Andrei, in remorse, asks whether he can find forgiveness for killing a man. Theophanes replies that God will forgive. But how long will the Tartar depredations last? 'Forever.' Back in the centre of the ruined church, the simpleton girl mournfully plaits the hair of a dead companion. Roublev resolves on a vow of silence. Snow begins to fall in the nave.

Episode VI: The Silence, 1412. A famine rages in the land. A poor pilgrim appears at the door of the Andronikov monastery and begs to be taken back. It is Kyril. He is given his old cell, but must

The sack of the cathedral: Theophanes the Greek

write out the scriptures fifteen times. Meanwhile Andrei has taken the simpleton girl under his protection. A party of mounted Tartars pass by. The girl emerges from a barn and starts flirting with them. She tries on a helmet, and looks at her reflection in a breastplate. The men feed her with meat meant for the hounds. Andrei attempts to protest, but his mortification is silent and helpless. They take her away with them on their horses.

Seventh and final episode. Eleven years later (1423). The great scene of the casting of the bell. The long (40-minute) sequence begins with a small band of soldiers scouring the countryside to find the bell-maker Nikolai. At the door of his cabin, the man's son Boriska (a boy of about 14, played by Nikolai Burlyaev, who played the hero of *Ivan's Childhood*) informs them that his father is dead. On an impulse he calls after them as they are about to ride off that he himself possesses his father's skills. The men shrug, but take him along with them.

Andrei and Kyril, meanwhile, passing a group of men and women, are recognised by the now tongueless jester, who for some reason thinks Andrei responsible for his betrayal to the soldiers all those years previously. Kyril intervenes to save Andrei from being hurt, and in the aftermath repents of his pride and begs Andrei to continue painting.

Cameos: the boy Boriska searches with his companions for the right clay for the firing, finding it eventually, by accident, at the bottom of a mud bank. (Andrei watches this in the rain from the other side of the river.) Scenes of the construction of the bell: the boy's imperiousness; minor mutinies among his assistants. At last, the great night-time moment of the casting. (Boriska has requisitioned all the silver from the Duke's coffers.) Later, the cast has set, the clay coating been peeled. The Grand Duke rides out with visiting ambassadors. As the clapper is levered toward the lip, the huge bell rings out with a true and clear tone.

In the excitement which follows, Andrei discovers the boy weeping in the mud. The secret slips out: Boriska had been lying about inheriting his father's skills and had never known the formula for the alloy. Yet the 'miracle' he has performed breaks the spell of Andrei's sadness. The vow of silence has run its course and it seems he may speak again.

We now move into the glorious concluding meditation. A brazier suddenly turns into colour. The charcoal transmutes into fragments of charred icons. Slowly these turn into the paintings of Andrei Roublev. At first they are shown 'abstractly', in close-up, but we gradually come to identify individual images: a church; a donkey; a vision of Christ; a scene of the disciples in the garden; Mary Magdalene stretched out on the ground; a dove ascending to Heaven; Judas; the manger with Mary and the animals; finally the great blue, yellow and pink geometrics of the icon of the Holy Trinity itself.

Not quite all, however, for Tarkovsky moves back to a vision of his beloved horses, running free in the rain in a meadow. Unambiguous images of freedom, release, happiness.

In *Sculpting in Time*, Tarkovsky speaks about the film's moral schema. It was meant to dramatise, he says, a relationship between virtue known intellectually and virtue known in the heart (or 'in practice'). Andrei, taught by Sergius' precepts, goes out from his monastery into the world. Shocked by reality, he loses his faith. Later, suffering, he finds it again, no longer this time as precept, but as lived and experienced truth. This truth he now bears as it were 'on his back' – irrefutably, and with authority. In a characteristic image, Tarkovsky declares that the discursive-didactic premise of the film needs to be 'burnt up in its own atmosphere', emerging finally from the ashes as a 'transparent clarity of the heart'.

How far Tarkovsky succeeds in effecting this aim lucidly is for the individual viewer to decide. It seems reasonable, however, at this stage, to point out a certain formal difficulty. As summarised in Tarkovsky's schema, we are dealing with a single man's destiny: the particular moral history of a chosen protagonist. But *Andrei Roublev* is only marginally 'narrative'. It seems more accurate to think of it as a historical fresco. The episodic nature of its construction constantly disperses the action outwards towards other incidents, other contexts, other meditations. Roublev under this aegis could be seen not so much as the actor of the events of the drama, as their spectator. And this would connect with another feature of the film that a number of people have found trouble with: the physical anonymity of the hero, which is such as to make it difficult to identify with him. (Early in the film Theophanes the Greek, we remember, mistakes Kyril for Andrei: probably a mistake that anyone could make.) Surely, we say, without this possibility of identification, the moral force of Andrei's redemption is in danger of becoming evaporated.

The difficulty that is touched upon here is one that recurs elsewhere in Tarkovsky's cinema. It can be put at its simplest by

The anonymity of Roublev: Andrei and the simpleton

saying that, in Tarkovsky's work, there is an inherent alliance
between the virtues of goodness and passivity. 'Hardness is closest
to death': the line from his father's poem that will be spoken in
voice-over in *Stalker* is felt, intuitively, as early as this. But
meekness is by definition difficult to dramatise. In *Andrei Roublev*
the inborn bias in narrative towards incisiveness of gesture and
command is refused – we must assume deliberately.

   To dwell on this for a little. Other film-makers have dramatised
goodness, some of them directors whom Tarkovsky admired
explicitly. One finds the character of St Francis in Rossellini's
Francesco, giullare di Dio (1950), for example, imbued with a kind
of non-problematic Christian cheerfulness that is both transparent
and dramatically successful. Again, in Buñuel's masterly *Nazarin*
(1959), the Spanish director's ironic malice becomes stopped short
in front of his own surprised admiration for the priest's heroism.
(It is a Christian film, forged at the last moment out of its maker's
atheism.) In Bresson's *Journal d'un curé de campagne* (1951),

43

finally, the priest-protagonist's virtue is allied, when the moment comes, to the fiercest pugnacity and will power. In each of these films by directors admired by Tarkovsky the emptying of the self in submission to God paradoxically enforces, not weakens, the hero's coherence of character. These protagonists are memorable and individualist. Yet Andrei remains vague, or anonymous.

I don't want to force a false answer out of this problem (which may not, after all, be felt by all viewers to be such). A few words can be said, however, about Tarkovsky's ethics of representation. One of the great tasks of the painter of the human form is to find for his subject the appropriate level of expressive facial gesture. If we may put it like this: the face can't afford to look as if it gives everything away at first glance. Tarkovsky speaks in *Sculpting in Time* of the dislike he harbours towards even painters like Raphael, whose overexpressive Sistine Madonna he contrasts with the gravity of Leonardo's mysterious Ginevra da Benci. (This latter painting makes a significant appearance in *The Mirror*.) What Tarkovsky likes about Leonardo's portrait is precisely its visual ambiguity: at different times, he says, 'either virtue or malice' can be read in the woman's reserved, unsoliciting self-possession. And in some way or other this is what Tarkovsky aims at for his own characters. For reasons of his own he is happy for his audience not to know, or to guess, too much about Roublev's 'inner' psychology.

The problem remains that the definition of Andrei is sometimes less clear than it might be. If we think, for example, of the conversations with Theophanes (surely a vital part of the film's logic), what point exactly is being made? The two men discuss the relationship of the Russians to the Tartars, but in terms so elliptical as to leave it unresolved which of the two men is more exigent and judgmental. Now it so happens that in the first draft of the film – the draft that became the basis of the 'literary scenario' published in France in 1970* – the pair are much more sharply contrasted. Theophanes stands for an Olympian distancing from the surrounding horrors, maybe even a cynicism towards them. The tenderness of Roublev is always to be asking why such horrors happen, and, by implication, to hope for a gradual amelioration. The nadir of his spiritual pilgrimage is by this token much clearer in the published scenario. It is the second meeting with Theophanes, the moment when, after the sacking of Vladimir, he himself gives up hope for the future of the Russian people. And

*Editeurs Français Réunis

44

just because *that* unhappiness is clearer, so the corresponding emergence from gloom – Andrei's salvation – becomes more poignant and artistically intelligible.

In an interview with Michel Ciment published in *Positif* in 1969, Tarkovsky defended the admitted narrative obscurity of *Andrei Roublev* by reference (of all allusions) to Engels. It was Engels' belief that the higher the cultural level of a work of art, the more 'disguised' it would be in its formal strategies. The artist, if he has a proper tact, does not want his best lines put in the mouth of a single character. How far he goes in evening out and distributing particular strands of argument, without denying the essential dramatic conflict, is one of the most delicate problems he has to deal with. And it is possible to say that in *Andrei Roublev* Tarkovsky hasn't quite solved it.

Against these considerations, however, one has to insist on the truly astonishing work of art that *Andrei Roublev* is. What is it that makes it so powerful, allows us to come away refreshed from each viewing? Above all, it seems to me, it is the film's uncompromised spiritual authenticity. There had been Russian works in the past that had made reference to religion, even sympathetically (one thinks of Eisenstein's *Ivan the Terrible*). But *Andrei Roublev* as far as I know is the first and maybe (for the time being) the last Russian film to look at the historical culture of Christianity not in terms of a so-called 'reactionary' content, but in terms of its own profound inner rightness and grandeur. How this came about can only be a matter of guesswork. Presumably the authorities felt that a 'humanist' Roublev – a secular artist who in articulating his own vision spoke for his people in the way that Soviet artists are supposed to – would emerge from the false social background. But if this was their hope they miscalculated. For it is tolerably plain that the knowledge of Christianity shown in the film is not merely a knowledge of pageant (as it is, I think, for all its glory, in *Ivan the Terrible*), but a profound inner moral knowledge which can only have come from years of preparation. We tend to forget how much – how programmatically – communism hates religion. The wise Pushkin spoke, however, of 'reigning religion' as 'the unfailing source of poetry in all peoples'. At its deepest level Tarkovsky agrees with that. Culture and religion *belong* to each other, indeed are each other. It is the single most daring proposition in *Andrei Roublev*.

Is there really, if one thinks about it, a 'problem of drama' in the film? The canvas is bristling and dynamic. In *Andrei Roublev*

Space, movement: the Tartars at the cathedral gates

space, movement and costume are used as they ought to be in cinema. The epic battles in films like *War and Peace* (1956), *Cleopatra* (1963), *The Fall of the Roman Empire* (1963) try to capture the sustained fury of old master paintings. Their limitation becomes apparent with the scenes which do *not* portray battles. One experiences a weariness amounting almost to melancholy at the elaborate processions of pomp and celebration belonging to the standard Hollywood epic (no matter how lavishly mounted). A heavy academic weight can be felt converting history into tableau, into waxwork. Authenticity of costume, and grandeur of set design, serve only to confirm how much such an aesthetics harks back to the world of an Alma Tadema, rather than to that of a Delacroix or a Rubens.

Now, to put it only at its most negative, the extras in *Andrei Roublev* avoid being afflicted by any such ant-like automatism. Tarkovsky's vital allegiance, actually, is to none of the artists just

46

named, but to Brueghel and Dürer. This means: every living corner of the canvas is animated. The distant individual incidents of a given scene seem to have the autonomy of such incidents in life, produced out of their own internal logic and necessity. Scenes, for example, surrounding the casting of the bell: the horseman in the far distance mounting the little hill, the dog pausing in the snow to scratch itself, the group of peasants huddled round the brazier; and beyond the peasants, the walls of the city itself (a 'real' city, not a city made out of balsa wood). It is the unforced and casual amplitude of scenes like this, bustling with energy, that impresses so much, coupled with the camera's ability to appropriate the landscape in whichever direction it finds itself turning. There it is: an entire world, ontologically indivisible, fantastically imagined. The majority of film-makers can only set up the conditions of truth in close-up and medium shot. Such truth of course also interests Tarkovsky. But scale, in *Andrei Roublev*, is heroic: it belongs to the inch and to the mile.

Let us return for a moment to this problem of 'obscurity'. The narrative is fragmentary, but not, in essentials, incoherent. What symbolism the film possesses springs, as we have said, from a shared public remembrance of Christianity. And then again, because such symbolism *is* public, Tarkovsky is relieved of having to insist on it portentously. Take the case of the bell in the seventh episode. As an image of renewal and hope its significance, plainly, does not have to be underlined. Yet it is not, somehow, as a 'symbol' that the image is still resonating in the mind after we have come out of the cinema. The construction of the bell, witnessed down to the smallest detail, forces the emphasis on to its material weight and physicality. The symbol is first and foremost an object. And this is true about all the objects, all the tactile physical presences in the film. (A point to recall is that in the Soviet Union, as opposed to Poland, church bells are not now usually rung.)

Another example might be the opening sequence of the balloon man making one of those first primitive efforts at flight. Originally, Tarkovsky tells us, the contraption was designed by him and Konchalovsky to have wings. Yet he obscurely felt that the matter, left like that, would be unsatisfactory. With wings goes an imagery – of Icarus, of Lucifer – that is simply too symbolically explicit. Tarkovsky's tact in substituting for the wings a rag-made balloon is, I think, the tact of a genuine artist.

The balloon flight in fact is so remarkable cinematically that we ought to push our examination of it a bit further. One assumes such an incident is anachronistic (manned flight was not invented till the 18th century), yet the viewer is struck not so much by the historical anomaly, as by the scene's boldness and deft poetic clarity. Coming right at the beginning of the film, it is excused the strict demands of verisimilitude (demands which would have operated were the incident embedded in the narrative). That the dream of flight, rather than flight itself, has always existed is indisputable; and along with the dream, numerous unknown or forgotten catastrophes in essence not different from the one Tarkovsky dramatises. The prologue works to establish an instant of history when science emerges, as it were, out of magic. The rightness of the scene is connected once again with matters of scale and cinematic enterprise – the film's opening out on to a vast panorama, a landscape. What we can see from the balloon is the *emptiness* of Russia, the endless unpopulated plains cut through by shining meandering rivers, a landscape in which cities aren't larger than villages (yet, in the native stone architecture of the churches, villages of extraordinary beauty). The 'crane shot' – the aerial perspective – has been used again and again as an establishing device in classic world cinema; but, either through lack of ambition or lack of funds, it seems increasingly in modern cinema in danger of neglect. Tarkovsky reminds us, as he did with the opening scenes of *Ivan's Childhood*, of the vertigo shot's great artistic value and effectiveness.

Yet another, final example of Tarkovsky's natural iconic power, this time from ground level: the film's beautiful meditation on horses. The equestrian scenes in *Andrei Roublev* owe everything to the example of Kurosawa, and it is only right in passing to pay homage to the Japanese master. *Rashomon* (1950), *The Seven Samurai* (1954) and *Throne of Blood* (1957) provided Tarkovsky in the late 1950s with an essential vocabulary and imagery. But taking over from Kurosawa, Tarkovsky extends the meditation. We could put it like this: if in past ages the presence of the horse lent dignity and elevation to the work of painters and sculptors, and if likewise, in literature, the subject of the epic is hard to imagine outside the context of the mounted, plumed, helmeted warrior, so the mastery and knowledge which this implies is kept alive now, if it is kept alive anywhere, above all in cinema. In *Andrei Roublev* there are wonderful cameos of animals, as noble and mysterious as anything in Rubens or Géricault. One thinks of the scene of the treacherous Prince Yuri racing the Tartar chieftain across the plains in front of Vladimir (there is an orientalism of composition

48

here worthy of Delacroix). Later, in the siege, we find an extraordinary shot of a motionless horse in the right foreground of the picture, calmly impervious to the fury of the surrounding battle. In the same sequence a horse and its rider mount the wooden steps of the belfry before crashing terribly to the corpse-strewn battleground. There is an unfetched magnificence in these images that needs no further comment. The horse is both animal and emblem. The poetic belongs to the concrete, and the two strands are inseparably fused.

Poetic emblems, then, are 'simultaneously' objects of nature. The demands of filming another historical epoch act as a lever against excessive esotericism. The very costumes of the warriors partake of this realist economy: independent blazons of magnificence, but simultaneously heavy armour to encase the body, subjecting it to the effects of heat, weight, discomfort.

In an essay on *Andrei Roublev,** Ivor Montagu wrote: 'Never have I seen so extraordinary and seamless a conjunction of period and nature; buildings, people, clothing, fields and weather.' This would seem essentially the right emphasis. Tarkovsky speaks of *Andrei Roublev* as a 'film of the earth'. Earth and country: in Russian as in other European languages the two words are the same. There are everywhere memorable telluric images: the mud of the riverbank on to which the forlorn pilot crashes; or the sodden midden in which the drunken peasants brawl in the jester episode; or the hill down which Boriska slithers in the pouring rain before making his discovery of the clay. Such imagery is sufficiently complicated. There is a metaphor here for the bleakness and horror of the times Tarkovsky is representing. But it also stands legitimately for the opposite: soaked in water, mud of course has positive, fecund possibilities (like the clay which forms the cast of the bell). Water in Tarkovsky is everywhere life-giving: most of all, paradoxically, in the vicinity of death. As one of the workmen in the ambush episode falls dying, the stream mingles with his paints, covering its surface with a milky pale translucence. Later, the image is taken up when the molten white alloy slips down the runnels into the bell cast. Water and rain; making and moulding. The bell begins to be built as the snows are clearing, and is completed a year later as they melt again. Thus it is as if the whole film is conceived of within the compass of the natural cycle. Only the really great film-makers can do this: Mizoguchi, Renoir,

Sight and Sound, Spring 1973.

Kurosawa, Dovzhenko. In the midst of the frequently terrible events which *Andrei Roublev* dramatises, the depiction of the rhythm of the seasons is the film's fine calmness and optimism.

Tarkovsky and Eisenstein

Tarkovsky's published statements about Eisenstein are a bit ambivalent. It is clear that he recognises his greatness. But his Russian master is Dovzhenko (the great poet of nature); Eisenstein is too obviously 'theatrical'. Early in *Sculpting in Time*, Tarkovsky concedes that *Ivan the Terrible* is 'impressive' without allowing that this 'huge day-time opera' had any appreciable influence on the making of *Andrei Roublev*. The hesitation is principally, I think, a technical one: it attaches to the earlier film-maker's doctrine of montage. In Bazinian terms, Tarkovsky's allegiance is to sequence not cutting, as we see from the prolonged mobile camerawork of *Andrei Roublev*. Cutting is disliked both for its innate ideological didacticism and also for its tendency towards incoherence. The famous passage of the battle on the ice in *Alexander Nevsky* is marred, says Tarkovsky, by its 'geographical vagueness'. The fighting is all rapid, fragmentary and repetitious; nothing is extended, watched, experienced deeply inside the frame. Rather similar is the ideological objection, Tarkovsky continues: montage 'buttonholes' the audience, converts serious-ness into satire and metaphor. Why should the audience be *told* that Kerensky resembles a peacock (to cite a justly famous scene from *October*)? Such insistence is importunate, inartistic.

Points likes these can be well made, yet leave the filmgoer feeling that something is being left unsaid. Is it just my own conviction that *Ivan the Terrible* is one of the grandest ever historical films which urges me, despite everything, to connect it to *Andrei Roublev*? Seeing Eisenstein's film is to be reminded first of all of its astonishing moral audacity. The portrayal of tyranny is unequi-vocal. It speaks from the heart and personality: it decisively belongs *inside* culture, as *Andrei Roublev* does.

Stylistically, *Andrei Roublev* and *Ivan the Terrible* are different; but there are similarities, maybe even references. I list them in no particular order. 1. The raid on Kazan, a central episode in *Ivan Part I*, bears similarities to the raid on Vladimir. Eisenstein, like Tarkovsky, is strongly attracted by the East, by the Orient; by the magnificence of war, as well as its terror. 2. The 'flashback' sequence of the reconciliation between Vassily and Yuri. Here the lenses magnify the faces of Yuri's followers, so that they loom over

Echoes of Eisenstein: Boriska presents the bell

their master portentously – an Eisensteinian moment of caricature.
3. By the same token both films share an interest in treachery and
remorse. This 'great Russian theme' is the central motor of
Pushkin's *Boris Godunov*, whose operatic version by Mussorgsky
was staged by Tarkovsky at Covent Garden in 1983. 4. The
Italian ambassadors riding out to inspect the bell recall the Polish
and Lithuanian ambassadors in *Ivan*. Both directors have a more
than passing eye for, and tolerance of, dandyism. 5. *Ivan the
Terrible* and *Andrei Roublev* are both black and white films which
erupt towards the end in spectacular colour. 6. Finally, there is a
shared interest in the imperiousness of children. Boriska's *hauteur*
harks back to the hero of *Ivan's Childhood*. Unforgettable scenes in
Part II of *Ivan the Terrible* show the infant Tsar on his throne,
surrounded by quarrelling Boyars, learning cunning and disdain
through his innocence. (It should be remembered that Part II of
Ivan the Terrible was first shown in Russia in 1959; that is, in
Tarkovsky's last year at film school.)

Summing up, we could say this: the two artists share an attitude towards the Middle Ages that is extraordinary for its robust tender appreciation. Both artists argue that, for all the horror of the times, men were more at home in the universe than they are now. And as so many decisions were literally matters of life and death, the soul became freed from triviality. Meanwhile (as perhaps never again) art, culture and the graces of life mysteriously flourished.

Icons

I have briefly talked about the actor's features in relation to traditional Western painting (Raphael, Leonardo). But one might wonder whether *Andrei Roublev* is not also an attempt at moments to reproduce the conditions and achievements of the most ancient of all Russian art forms, the icon. There are immediate theological objections: perhaps, in their literalness, insuperable. It isn't obviously a matter of surface similarity. An icon is an object of religious veneration, whereas a film is 'merely' a work of art. The camera constantly moves, queries, sets up relationships; the icon inspires devotion from its stillness.

But Tarkovsky, too, is interested in stillness. And if there is a sensible claim to be made it is surely here: Tarkovsky's facial portraits (Ivan, Daniel, Theophanes), like Roublev's portraits of Christ and the saints, are concerned with the expression of noble, inner rapture. The piercing gaze of the cinema is not, primarily, in Tarkovsky's work, the search for psychological truth, so much as a search for what he terms 'spirituality'. He seeks out the evidence, in the human, of the divine.

These of course are delicate matters. Do we in the West believe in the divine any longer? Is it within the power of art to *revive* belief in it? Since these are among the most important questions one can ask about Tarkovsky's cinema, I shall come back to them again.

SOLARIS

Solaris appears to be the film that Tarkovsky was least happy with; he gave little space to it in his book. There were apparently difficulties with the leading actors, Natalya Bondarchuk, daughter of Tarkovsky's great enemy Sergei (the film director), and Donatas Banionis (whom he found unresponsive). Stanislaw Lem, the Polish author of the book on which the film was based, came near to disowning the film version. Memories of these quarrels obviously left a feeling of unhappiness. It is further reported that Tarkovsky was not pleased with the ending, finding it too obviously symbolic (the image is that of the Return of the Prodigal Son). Beyond this, we sense an uneasiness in his public utterances about the genre of science fiction itself. He saw it as an artificial construct, too distant from his essential humanistic concerns.

I must say immediately that these are not opinions I share. *Solaris* seems to me in every way a majestic and achieved work of art: not to make too fine a point of it, a masterpiece. I have seen the film several times, and am struck each time anew not only by its plastic beauty, but by its quality of thoughtfulness, the density of its poetic meditation. Behind its fantastic exterior and subject matter, there is a quiet and philosophical human truthfulness.

Solaris is a work of Russian science fiction. The concept is perhaps already an odd one for Westerners, who mostly continue to imagine Soviet art within the limits of socialist realism. One of the striking aspects of *Solaris* is the full-scale confidence of its imagery. The film is mounted in colour and widescreen. Like *Andrei Roublev* it was evidently, by Russian standards, an expensive venture. Its high standard of craftsmanship makes it comparable to contemporary Western science fiction films. *Solaris* emerged three years later than Kubrick's *2001: A Space Odyssey* (1968), but the actual imagery of the computerised technology involved in spaceship living is – within important qualifications which I shall specify – not so very different between the two movies. (It may have been naive of me to imagine that it should be. I am talking about design and art direction. As far as real space research is concerned, the USSR has always been as ambitious as the

United States. At nineteen billion dollars a year – in 1985 – against civilian NASA's 8 billion, Russia in fact spends over twice as much money as the USA.)

We could push these speculations a bit further. There is a sense in which, in looking at any Russian film, we in the West are ourselves engaged in an activity that has some parallels with the world of science fiction. For Tarkovsky's speculations about the unknown – the outside, the Other – provide a curious mirror (henceforward a key image in Tarkovsky's cinema) to our own speculations about Russia. Just as I say, people tend to think of the country as backward and scientifically inefficient; but here in *Solaris* the tele-machines work smoothly, the electric doors whirr open on to vistas of technology, the teak conference tables are massive and solid. Instead of looking like dull apparatchiks, the space officials are relaxed and smartly dressed. Is Russia so different from us? How is it different? The film brings up these thoughts as we watch it.

A deeper regard, however, will show that the emphasis on technology is already misleading. For the truly great boldness of this film about space exploration is exactly how relaxed, and I would even say sceptical, it is about the ultimate importance of such undertakings. In the late 1960s when the film was embarked on, the Soviet Union and the United States had reached a vitally important stage in their space programmes; but, as in all Tarkovsky's films, there is absolutely no intrusion of state propaganda. The intensity of the film-maker's private artistic concerns seals out any official interstate competitiveness. In a speech of amazing independence the scientist Kelvin muses that if there is one reason for going up into space, it is so that we can look back again on Earth with renewed understanding and tenderness. The whole 'adventure' of space is regarded sceptically. The film seems to say that our destiny is on this planet or nowhere.

In keeping with this, the first third of *Solaris* is set firmly on earth, much of it in Kelvin's dacha and wild spacious garden. (This is an addition to Lem's novella.) The house's old wooden appliances, the prints on the walls depicting eighteenth-century balloons, the busts of philosophers, the cut flowers in the vases, the horse gambolling outside in the meadow, all establish for the film a terrain of memory, a human landscape of loved things to be looked back on with longing and desire. Ancestral images: images of the past in a film about the future.

Solaris: Kelvin on the space-platform

Narrative

The film's narrative, adapted by Tarkovsky and F. Gorenstein
from the Lem novel, starts with the following situation. A number
of years ago a strange planet in the form of a sea of liquid gas
intruded itself into the solar system, parking itself outside the
atmosphere but within space-travelling vicinity of the earth.
Expeditions investigated it, somewhat inconclusively. 'Solaristics'
became in due course a run-down science. On one of these visits
some years before the film begins, the cosmonaut Burton (Vladislav Dvorzhetsky) had got into trouble: two of his co-pilots,
descending from the spaceship into the gas ocean, had failed to
return. Burton, diving in to rescue them, had encountered strange
sights – an enchanted garden and a plaster-cast replica of a
monstrous baby. Were these the visions of a man whose mind had
been 'turned' by the danger, or the authentic sighting of real
objects? The authorities remain baffled and mistrustful.

Now, however, the sea is becoming mysteriously active again. Another cosmonaut, Kris Kelvin (Donatas Banionis), an acquaintance of Burton, is detailed to investigate. Kelvin plans an expedition from his father's dacha. There is much self-questioning about its purpose, during which Kelvin quarrels with Burton (for he may have to close the station down). Finally, however, there is a semi-reconciled leave-taking.

Kelvin's self-piloted rocket sets him down on the space platform hovering above Solaris. Here he meets the two long-serving scientists, Snauth (Yuri Jarvet) and Sartorius (Anatoly Solonitsin). We soon learn that a third scientist, Gibaryan (Sos Sarkissian), an old friend of Kelvin, has committed suicide, leaving behind a video-tape giving an account of fears and premonitions. The platform is run-down and isolated. As a companion, Snauth is scarcely communicative. Sartorius is depressive, perhaps mad.

Immediately Kelvin arrives he is greeted by hauntings and apparitions. His deceased wife Hari (Natalya Bondarchuk) emerges out of nowhere, apparently ready to take up the relationship. He puts her in a rocket in a panic and sends her, as he thinks, back to earth. But the same night she reappears and climbs into his bed. Next morning, as he leaves her to find his colleagues, the room in which they have been sleeping explodes. Hari, though injured, 'reconstitutes' herself immediately. The woman appears to be made (so the other scientists suggest) out of neutrinos, stabilised by the vicinity of Solaris – normal in everything except her atomic constitution, and her amnesia.

As Hari and Kelvin converse, details of Kelvin's past life, including discreditable episodes, are presented to us. There had been quarrels and periods of unhappiness. Finally he had left her, triggering her suicide by a poison syringe.

The scientists (Sartorius especially) become hostile to Hari's presence, believing that the developing relationship impedes their primary task of making contact with the planet. Hari overhears Snauth discussing ways in which she can be disposed of. At Snauth's birthday party in the spaceship library she tearfully defends her integrity, saying that she suffers like a normal human being. But Kelvin himself no longer needs to be convinced that Hari really is his wife in everything that matters; while Snauth, who is drunk or ill, comes round to admitting that positivistic science has its limitations.

From here on, reality becomes increasingly confused. In a

beautiful sequence of weightlessness Hari and Kelvin levitate while musing on a painting of Brueghel, whose snow-covered landscape reminds them of their life on earth. But there is still a central agony to the relationship. Hari's existence as a neutrino woman confines her to the spaceship; the realisation of this cruel fact causes her to commit suicide again, by drinking liquid oxygen. Unable to die, she once more comes back to life. (Snauth comments sardonically: 'I can't get used to these constant resurrections!') Kelvin places her on the bed and nurses her. Now it is his turn to become delirious. In his illness he dreams that his mother and Hari, the earth and the spaceship, all become confused and interchangeable. On waking, he is confronted by Snauth who tells him that Hari is no longer with them; indeed, that she will never come back (he reads out a letter of farewell).

Meanwhile, Snauth says, islands of matter have appeared on the great gas ocean in response to increasing doses of radiation. The 'breakthrough' looks as if it is coming. Should Kelvin stay, or return to earth? He muses on the question in a melancholy final monologue. Why return to earth? Better to 'stay here among things we both have touched, which remember our presence. For what? In the hope that she will return? I have no such hope. The one thing left is to wait; yet for what, I don't know. For new miracles?'

The film ends with a vision of Kelvin meeting his father at the dacha, throwing himself on his knees in a gesture of repentance. The camera at this moment moves off into the air to reveal the dacha on an island surrounded by water: not Earth at all, but the Sea of Solaris. Has he stayed (as he said he would)? Or has he in fact returned to humanity?

Physics and metaphysics
If the film shares with Lem's novel the central tenets of its narrative, it forges whatever profundity it possesses by specifically filmic means. Its central truth (for convenience, the film's 'metaphysics') belongs to the cinema – belongs,that is to say, to the play of light over canvas, to the movement and stillness of actors, to that combination of music, set design and colour which differentiates a film from the printed word of literature.

The central conceit of the film – that the character Hari can be 'reconstituted' out of neutrinos – provides Tarkovsky with a way of looking at a crisis in a relationship. It is a love affair he examines, seen under the auspices of regret. The film provides the postmortem on an episode that went wrong, perhaps because of certain

A dream of reconciliation: Hari and Kelvin

actions that were in retrospect avoidable, but which nevertheless remains the central fact in either participant's existence. The film, so to speak, dreams a kind of utopian reconciliation between Kelvin and Hari. But its power to move us (in fact its greatness, even its tragedy) lies in the way Tarkovsky simultaneously lets it be known that such healings are, in the world of men, unattainable.

Meanwhile there is the image of love itself, of what love *should* be, brought before us on the screen in gestures of memorable tenderness. Crucial to the nobility of the film is the fact that not only does Kelvin love Hari but she, with an even stronger woman's passion, still loves him. Her forgiveness matches – cancels out – his guilt and desertion. Actually there is not even a question of forgiveness, for Hari comes to Kelvin with the guilelessness and simplicity that is predicated by her amnesia. All ghosts in some way are forlorn; and if Hari's love for Kelvin is clear, convincing and human, everything else about her is vague, confused and pitiable. The film summons up, from such 'impossible' premises, gestures of love's mutual protectiveness that have rarely been equalled in modern cinema. The way that the lovers' hands touch and entwine, or a head lies on a pillow, or hair sticks to a tear-stained cheek – this tenderness between partners (before love has been corrupted by error or boredom) is *Solaris'* profound emotional truthfulness.

Behind this human bedrock, then, there follow the film's metaphysical speculations, foremost of which is a sort of abstract meditation on immortality. The mortuary slab on which the dead scientist Gibaryan lies (covered in icy plastic) is filmed in such a way as to bring to mind the other, conjugal, bed on which Kelvin and Hari sleep and dream. Is death a sleep? As long as there is someone to remember the dead under the aegis of those supreme emotions, longing and love, it can be said that immortality 'exists'.

In order to make this clearer (and yet at the same time more complicated), Tarkovsky makes fine use of film-within-film. From the early sequence where the youthful Burton looks back at his older ruined self from the widescreen wall monitor; to the middle scene in which the video of the dead Gibaryan addresses Kelvin from 'the far side of the grave'; to the central and profoundly moving sequence where Kelvin's own 'home video' shows Hari the image of herself as she was on earth near the snow-covered dacha – everything combines to demonstrate that memory need *not* be extinction; and that on the contrary we live in significance to the extent that we are prepared to embrace the shadows of our loss.

But isn't this also, really, the metaphysics of film itself? Derrida calls cinema the 'science of ghosts'. Those actors on screen (the big screen, not just the screen-within-a-screen), aren't they *also* present to us and absent at the same time? And isn't this in fact what makes the cinema often so poignant? Its present tense is so often also a past tense.

Actors

Tarkovsky had difficulty with some of his actors on the set of *Solaris* who constantly wanted to know what the film 'meant'. Yet I doubt whether these difficulties can be inferred from the finished performances, which harmonise well, and achieve the general level of seriousness Tarkovsky was aiming for. Yuri Jarvet, the Estonian actor playing Snauth (he was a fine King Lear in Kozintzev's 1971 film), provides, effortlessly enough, the leaven of sardonic humour without which a film like *Solaris* might easily have frozen into solemnity. His eccentricity is complicated (not mechanical). Banionis (Kelvin) was the major problem: previously he had been exclusively a stage actor, and wanted, in the traditional theatrical way, to possess a conception of his complete role before the filming began, a request which Tarkovsky – sculptor and mosaicist as much as *metteur en scène* – found impossible to oblige. Not that it matters in the event. The actor has a dark, troubled integrity which convinces.

All the additional parts are good. Solonitsin, as Sartorius, taps levels of fierceness – perhaps one should say cussedness – that were beyond his reach in the altogether 'milder' role of Roublev. Sartorius, of course, stands for the intransigence of science, but in Solonitsin's hands the role isn't caricatured. Likewise, Vladislav Dvorzhetsky is an excellent gloomy Burton. The father, in the dacha scenes, is played by Nikolai Grinko, an old and trusted comrade of the director.

Above all, there is Natalya Bondarchuk. The actress expresses the pathos of Hari's plight with supreme tenderness. It must have been difficult, with the film's resurrections, not to have made her playing ridiculous. Yet in two scenes in particular Tarkovsky extracts from her features the unpastiched purity of great fifteenth-century painting. I am thinking of the moment in the home videotape when, after numerous shots of Kelvin's mother in the snow-bound landscape, Hari appears for the first time as Kelvin's wife. Outside the dacha, she turns to smile sadly towards the camera: towards *herself* watching the tape in Kelvin's bedroom. What profound melancholy and suffering is implied in her inexpressive subtle gaze. And conversely, what fine serenity attaches to the sequence of the birthday party, where Hari floats effortlessly in her lover's arms. These are only two of the daring moments which make *Solaris* linger long in the memory.

Correspondences

Blake said, 'We murder to dissect', and Tarkovsky would have agreed. A work of art ought to resist being cut up into component parts in order to demonstrate a unity which is felt by the viewer instinctively. I have spoken in a previous chapter about poetic correspondences, and without going into the vexed question of how intentionally such correspondences are planted (a maybe impossible task), *Solaris* may be commended as one of the richest of all Tarkovsky's works in the intensity of its visual rhyming. There is a specific support for this in the narrative. Tarkovsky, of

Natalya Bondarchuk as Hari

course, is intent on showing us the mirror-like interdependence of earth and of space – in the last resort one and the same location, filtered through the human imagination.

Such connections can be traced through a number of linked images. The opening shot of the film shows us the lake in the neighbourhood of Kelvin's dacha. Underneath the water, gentle fronds of algae weave to and fro (a Bach chorale prelude on the soundtrack). The image is picked up in the film on numerous occasions: for example, in the two or three moments when the camera focuses on the hair of the sleeping Hari, spread out in baroque curlicue on the pillow of Kelvin's bed, or frozen fantastically on the floor by the liquid oxygen. At other times the camera picks up the tassles of Hari's knitted woollen shawl, linking them metonymically to her coiffure. A further instance is the pieces of paper cut into strips and hung beside the breeze from the air conditioner (an ingenious sound-device fashioned by Snauth to imitate the rustling of leaves back on earth). Perhaps most extraordinary of all is the zoom close-up on to Kelvin's face, not stopping at a recognisable profile but moving beyond, to come to rest on his earlobe; or to be more precise, on the little tufts of hair growing out of it.

What is the significance of these images? The initial fronds of algae are wonderfully restful shapes in themselves. We have all stared into those ponds in our childhood. The submarine vegetation caressed by water weaves a musical harmony as if under its own living impulse. Conversely, the fronds of Hari's hair and Kelvin's earlobe become, on the giant cinemascope screen, a veritable landscape of nature. Objects become living organisms, as living organisms turn into objects. Everything in the universe 'belongs' finally to everything else.

To make this concrete, there are extraordinary substitutions of scale. The nebulous Sea of Solaris stands at one moment, externally, for the vast oceans of galaxies; at another moment, by microscopic inversion, for the millions of atoms of the human brain. One single beautiful sequence may be cited as bringing out these developing thoughts explicitly. Burton has angrily left Kelvin and is driving back into the city with his young son. The boy leans forward inside the car and rests his head against his father's back, an image of pacifying serenity. It is twilight on the motorway. The winking rear-lights of the cars on the slipways gradually transform in front of our eyes into a dance of the planets and galaxies. In the colossal shifts of space and scale – the exact contours of which are only a discovery of the last twenty years – Tarkovsky has found, it seems to me, a genuine fresh subject-matter for poetry.

Roundness, specularity

Does it mean much to contemplate the universe on film, in the way I am thinking of, poetically? All real thinking is bottomless, for it contains a kind of built-in tautology. To 'consider the universe' – the word 'consider' means, literally, 'look at the stars' – is to consider a problem which, solutionless, is obliged to be circular. Globes and circles in fact dominate the film's visual vocabulary. First there is the spaceship itself, a gyroscope turning on an axis (Snauth in a late scene sprints round its interior perimeter). The image is repeated in the portholes and in the round exit ramp of the shuttle-rocket. A round ball, sent spinning from out of nowhere, greets Kelvin as he steps on to the space platform. Later, in the splendidly decorated library, the table is circular, as is the fine crystal chandelier above it; meanwhile, the mirror directly outside Kelvin's quarters is circular and concave. Finally, of course, there is the Sea of Solaris itself, in panoramic master-shot, its surface distorted by innumerable swirling vortices.

Circularity: Kelvin and Snauth in the spaceship perimeter

In sequence after sequence, too, there is 'specularity'. I have
already mentioned the numerous scenes where a character looks at
himself in a video recording. Early in the film Burton, while
playing the tape of his questioning by the space authorities, is seen
to address observations – mainly of anger and disgust – to his
former and younger self, as if into some sort of time-mirror. There
are frequent moments that involve one or other of the characters
bending down to look through a glass panel, either outwards
(through the porthole on to Solaris), or inwards (for instance,
Kelvin looking through the dacha window at his father standing
rain-soaked at the stove).

Is it easy to say precisely what all this amounts to? There is the
obvious enough observation that it fictionalises the discourse;
holds it in perpetual inverted commas. Perhaps we can say,
though, that along with the standard or weaker meaning of

reflection goes the stronger: the mirrors are a vital part of the film's thoughtfulness. So much of the film is simply involved in looking, thinking, standing still – thought's power sent out and bounced back again, as it were. The film opens with a picture of the woods and the lake in early summer, and closes (or nearly closes) on the same tableau, frozen over, at winter time. In each case Kelvin is walking along the edge of the lake in silent contemplation. The interiority here is like a scene from an austere poem by Wordsworth. How often do we find such rapt intense stillness in films? No narrative at all.for the time being; simply a man, by himself, standing in the presence of nature, and *thinking*.

Dreyer's Ordet

Two or three times in *Solaris* we are present when Hari shudders back to life as if from an epileptic fit. The topos of the woman rising from the dead, like that of the puppet rising to life from the scientist's laboratory bench, has numerous distinguished precedents in the cinema. Sequences from Lang's *Metropolis* (1927), Whale's *Bride of Frankenstein* (1935), Powell and Pressburger's *Tales of Hoffmann* (1951) come to mind. In fact, there are too many to specify. But outside the specific genres of science fiction and horror, a comparable instance is the resurrection of the heroine Inger at the end of Dreyer's sublime masterpiece *Ordet* (1954). Since both Tarkovsky and Dreyer are operating at the very highest level of seriousness, a brief comparison between the two ways of treating the theme might be instructive.

Let me recapitulate the events leading up to the climax of *Ordet* ('The Word', from a play by Kaj Munk). The rich farmer's daughter Inger has died tragically in childbirth. Throughout the film we have observed at intervals the behaviour of her mad brother Johannes whose delusion is that he is the living Jesus Christ. With infinite patience Johannes' family put up with his ravings and mutterings (for this turn-of-the-century rural milieu is fiercely Christian and duty-bound). Finally as the family stand grieving round Inger's coffin, Johannes appears after an absence. At first his altered speech and more dignified bearing allow them to think that the madness has mercifully abated. Soon, however, he starts muttering about 'resurrection': he will bring the dead Inger back to life again. The family is naturally horrified; as is the pastor standing with them in the parlour, guardian of morals and orthodoxy. But in the sequence that follows, of almost unbearable pathos and strength, Dreyer chooses to show us the miracle

64

actually happening. The power of the madman's faith indeed brings the woman back to life again. She moves her fingers, opens her eyes and smiles. Everyone weeps (including the audience). The greatness of the film is at one and the same time to let us know that this resurrection is 'impossible', and to make us feel that the desire for it is the sublimest, most noble human impulse.

The sympathetic dramatisation of religious Hope makes the drama immediately Christian. At the same time, the very necessity for bringing the girl back to life can be made to look as if it speaks in another, non-religious accent. (For if there were a Heaven we would surely all be content to meet *there*.) *Solaris* doesn't talk about Heaven; as I have tried to bring out, it talks about immortality in human terms, linking it to memory and desire. The film avoids (unlike *Roublev* of course) a specifically religious symbolism. Again, a small difference: it is not Kelvin's faith which brings Hari back from the dead, but rather, in terms of the story, her *own* unrequited longing for *him*. The circumstances are such that the supreme test of faith belongs to the victim; and one doesn't really think of this as being 'Christian'.

Resurrection: Hari just before she reconstitutes herself

65

Fortunately, the truth of either film doesn't finally depend on such labelling. The test of their profundity lies elsewhere and in themselves. It is the fate of modern art, I think, to live in a sort of metaphysical ambiguity. If *Solaris* is friendly to religion, it does not finally reside *in* religion. No art can – not even works of devotion like *Andrei Roublev*. And this is probably as true for such profound seekers after the Absolute as Dreyer and Tarkovsky as it is for out-and-out atheists like Godard.

The figure of the mother

In the scene on the spaceship which incorporates shots from Kelvin's home video, Kelvin's elegant mother, a tall blonde woman (O. Yisilova), is linked to Hari by the strange patchwork dress both women wear; and also by the fact that they are shown at much the same age and against a similar romantic background (a snow-covered landscape). Even more explicitly, in Kelvin's later delirium, the mother and the wife become literally interchangeable. The scenes would seem to introduce a theme that henceforth has a certain place in Tarkovsky's work: we see it in *The Mirror* and again in *The Sacrifice*, and a variation on it (this time a wife converting into a possible mistress) in *Nostalghia*. We wonder how to make sense of it, above all aesthetically.

Tarkovsky in his public pronouncements tended to pour scorn on Freud and his legacy. Psychoanalysis, he maintained, was the key species of modern charlatanism, the enemy of the spirit. Yet the insistence of the image (in Freudian terms, its repetitive, obsessional quality) makes us ask whether there isn't an important psychological fixation buried at its root. It is a matter of record, for instance, how much Tarkovsky loved and honoured his mother, Maria. In fact, the original intention of *The Mirror* was to incorporate a 40-minute documentary interview with her, in which he would ask her about her life and struggles and opinions. This was to be filmed, we are told, without her knowledge, by recourse to three hidden cameras. The scenes were not in fact done; but, of the finished film, Tarkovsky often spoke of it establishing his mother's bona fides for 'immortality' – this with an emphasis and literalness that could raise eyebrows.*

A residue of unexplained autobiographical material is not

---

*In his last film, *The Sacrifice*, the long rambling monologue by Alexander in the Icelandic woman's bedroom privileges once again the protagonist's *mother* and *sister* over his wife (whom he appears rather to despise).

66

necessarily fatal to a work of art, even a public one like the cinema. Tarkovsky's work is, more than most film-makers', simultaneously autobiographical and oblique. The only task for the critic is to decide whether such material coalesces with the rest of the narrative. As it happens, I believe that the 'Oedipal' theme here does integrate perfectly well with the rest of the material. We may grasp its troublesomeness, even subliminally, as part of the film's overall authenticity.

Stanislaw Lem

Lem's novel was published in 1961. It is about 200 pages long. Tarkovsky and Gorenstein's work of adaptation (completed in May 1968) was firstly a matter of reducing the story's bulk, slicing out a large amount of detail. Perhaps the biggest single section to be dispensed with is an account of the history of 'Solaristics', for which Lem provides a cod-scientific résumé of the various theories held about the planet over the previous hundred years. The book is more concerned than the film with the nature of Solaris itself; and Lem spends long paragraphs describing the planet's rich, baroque metamorphoses.

As well as refining and cutting down, the film-makers made one or two significant additions. Lem's novel takes place entirely in space. The earth scenes in the dacha, so crucial in the film, are Tarkovsky's own. In general, the family element is decisively increased (it was going to be increased even more). The film gives Kelvin an adolescent daughter, and Burton a son (perhaps a grandson). The old-fashioned library, with its shelves of leather-bound volumes, is a feature shared by the book and the film; but the beautiful levitation scene which occurs there after Snauth's birthday party is an invention of the film. And so on.

On the whole, though, the film follows the book pretty faithfully, which makes Tarkovsky's falling out with Lem the more anomalous. There is a clutch of specific details that the adapter has taken over. To mention just a few: the odd string vest that Kelvin wears in the film beneath his leather jacket (it is worn in the book by Snauth); the strips of paper hanging near the ventilation shaft; the sardonic child's drawing of 'Humanity' pinned to Gibaryan's door; the strange little dwarf (or hint thereof) who seems to be keeping Sartorius company; even the shape of the sea itself, described in the book as 'thick foam, the colour of blood, which gathered in the troughs of the waves'; and later on 'like the crawling skin of an animal: the incessant, slow-motion contractions of muscular flesh secreting a crimson foam'. This is all safely in the film.

Are these instances trivial or important? If the film is a faithful adaptation, it is also in its essence profoundly different. The human sorrow, which Tarkovsky foregrounds, has only a minor place in the book. The grandeur of Tarkovsky's *Solaris* is, I think, an independent entity.

THE MIRROR

If I may start this chapter with a personal reminiscence. I remember vividly the excitement of my first viewing of *The Mirror*, long before I knew much about its director. The film was obscure in its incidents; many episodes were not, by conventional standards, properly explained. Yet even as I watched it, I felt possessed by the sensation that you occasionally come across in dreams, of an understanding so complete that you yourself become part of the dramaturgy. *Ignis fatuus* or the truth? This identification, I suppose, is a definition of the Aristotelian *aesthesis*, plainly an emotional rather than an intellectual understanding; yet so strongly experienced, perhaps, as to render the intellectual unimportant. Rationalisations could come afterwards (and they did). The deep structure of the film always seemed to me to be transparent.

In retrospect, one attempted to put its boldness into words. Why was the film so striking? It seems to me that two connected things can be said about it. Firstly, it is one of the rare completely achieved films of autobiography. Autobiography proper has tended to exist only on the fringes of cinema: certain American underground film-makers spring to mind who in the absence of funds (or perhaps merely in the absence of ambition) turn the camera, so to speak, on themselves. But *The Mirror*, despite being personal, speaks somehow with the authority of third-person narrative art. Autobiography in the film is woven into history, lending it a grandeur and a classicism. The film is profoundly intimate; yet not, in the last resort (as no real art ever can be), solipsistic.

Secondly (obvious enough, but it has to be said), this autobiography was coming out of Russia. True written autobiography, in novels and poetry, was rare enough as far as one knew in the Soviet Union. But a publicly conceived 'memoir-film', made by an artist who does not identify with the state, who was not finishing his career but rather (as he saw it) just commencing it: surely this was something unusual. It was this freedom of personal reminiscence more than anything which struck me when first watching the film.

Here it was in front of one's eyes, when one believed the authorities did not allow such things: a portrait of childhood that took its own path, established its own values, said what it wanted to with candour.

Later we discovered that the authorities were in fact far from happy with the outcome. They refrained from banning the film, instead placed it in 'Category 3', that of limited release, allowing it to be shown only in a few out of the way suburban cinemas. Meanwhile the director had been subjected to an inquisition by his peers. Goskino, the state cinema organisation, met the Union of Soviet Cinematographers in 1975 over a discussion of 'contemporaneity in the cinema'. The proceedings were published in the state cinema journal *Iskusstvo Kino*. Here *The Mirror* was criticised unambiguously, though more, it appears, in sorrow than in anger. V. N. Naumov (a film-maker): 'Many, including the most sophisticated viewers, couldn't make out what was happening on screen. It remained for them something mysterious, non-understandable.' Khutsiev: 'If I have to speak at the highest level – and I can't do anything less here – then I cannot consider the film a success. . . . For here we are talking about a master, an artist from whom I always expect original and profound thought, a serious dialogue with me, the viewer. In this film no dialogue takes place, only a monologue, in which the author, not caring about an interlocutor, talks only to himself. And that distresses one. I have an impression that Tarkovsky doesn't really care about how he is received even by the most sophisticated viewer.' Chukhrai (*Ballad of a Soldier*), more dogmatic and Stalinist: 'One must not orient oneself to some special kind of audience. Cinema art is an art of the masses. . . . And if the artist has something to say, he doesn't put his thought into code, he says what he thinks.' Other criticisms, from bureaucrats rather than film-makers, were, perhaps predictably, cruder in their envy, and blunter in their contempt for the film's 'elitism', its flouting of the positive socialist conventions.

In relaying fragments from the discussion, the writer here has to be careful: I may have missed, in the translated proceedings, certain aspects of its context and tone. Anyway, it may be asked whether the dislike evinced by Tarkovsky's peers is intrinsically any different from that articulated by Western authorities for certain types of minority Western cinema. Everyone knows the testiness that occasionally breaks out in the West between bull-headed producers and sensitive directors under their charge. Tarkovsky was not on trial for his life: that at least was different from the Stalin epoch. On the other hand, one probably shouldn't, either, go too far in the opposite direction. Herbert Marshall, from whose article* I have just quoted these verdicts, gives reasons for believing that the reception of the film went way beyond mere official 'disappointment'. Tarkovsky was publicly placed in a position not so very far from disgrace, and disgrace, in the Soviet Union, is absolute. As far as one knows, it was the reception accorded to *The Mirror* which finally alerted Tarkovsky to the need for survival, and the reluctant realisation that some day he might have to work elsewhere.

What was it that the assembled directors – some of them at least, like Yuli Raizman, sophisticated men and artists of distinction – found so forbidding? It surely can't have been the fact that the film splits up, unpredictably and without signalling its transitions, between present and past. The history of the cinema by now has sufficient examples of this juggling with time-scales not to upset the viewer unduly. *Hiroshima mon amour* is a celebrated instance. There is a film by Carlos Saura, *Dulces horas* (1981), which uses exactly the same freedoms as *The Mirror* to discuss past and present Spain in a way that only the most perverse critic would want to call difficult. I would go further and say: *The Mirror* is not even 'avant-garde' – at least in the way that the 20th century has accustomed us to make use of the term, as a sort of mocking flirtation with meaninglessness.

What was it, then, that was so foxing? Was it that criticism in the Soviet Union, after the years of experiment with socialism, had no adequate way of discussing the personal any more? Other aspects of life are debated the whole time with immense conscientiousness (social problems of alcoholism, flat shortages, bureaucracy). I would like to put forward in the following discussion a tentative answer to the authorities' scepticism.

The mirror and what it reflects

Mirrors seem intrinsic to cinema for some reason, and other directors besides Tarkovsky have explored their magic. The camera in a room will seek out the looking-glass to 'etherealise' a narrative, and give it a deeper dimension of meditation and strangeness.

The actual image of the mirror itself occurs on a number of occasions in Tarkovsky's film, as it appeared before in *Solaris*.

*'Andrei Tarkovsky's *The Mirror*', *Sight and Sound*, vol. 45 no. 2, Spring 1976.

The Mirror: 'a moment of memory and mystery'

Firstly there is the mystical flashback following the narrator's
father's return from a long absence, when Maria (Margarita
Terekhova), the narrator's mother, washes her hair in a basin.
Water streams down from the roof and the walls. She walks in an
'indoor storm' joyfully. We see her briefly in a full-length mirror:
then in another mirror at the other side of the room, her image
transformed into that of an old woman. A second instance is when
Natalia, the narrator's wife (Margarita Terekhova again, in her
'present-day' role), questions her husband about the reasons for
their marriage breaking up. Here the conversation is conducted as
she glances at herself in the looking glass, at one stage breathing on
it and rubbing out the moisture with her fingers. And later in the
film, too, there is a third flashback, which takes place during the
war, when the barefoot boy and his mother timidly arrive at a
neighbour's house in the country. While the mother goes into a
separate chamber to bargain with the neighbour about the selling
of her earrings, young Alexei is left alone in a room. It is twilight;

the paraffin lamp flutters and fails; the boy's face becomes intensely reflected in the glass hanging over the mantelpiece. It is a moment of memory and mystery.

These, if one can put it like this, are conventional mirror scenes; but in addition there are, as one would expect, a number of quasi-mirror scenes, where objects and faces are seen either obliquely, or refracted through glass. Polished and reflecting surfaces have, throughout, a sort of quiet underlining presence in the film, not so much symbolic as subliminal. What, then, do these mirrors and surfaces reflect? A connection between present and past, a connection of *stasis*. A vital belief in the film appears to be that nothing of importance ever changes. 'The table is the same for the grandfather and the grandson.' Not only *is* the same, but must be.

In so far as the film is 'subversive' in the authorities' terms, it is probably subversive, then, in the approval which it gives to this state of affairs, its scepticism about standard forms of improvement. A man's life exists, if it exists at all profoundly, in the continuity of one generation to the next. It is important to take in how firmly, almost literally, Tarkovsky believes in this. The house in the country where the early scenes of the film are shot is not only modelled on the house in which Tarkovsky was brought up, it was even constructed on the same spot of land. (Since the present-day owners of the land, a collective farm, concentrated their production on oats, Tarkovsky rented the neighbouring fields too, and sowed them a year before filming with the silky waving buckwheat he remembered from his childhood.) Sufficient openings here, one supposes, for subsequent irony: when the filming was over the 'house' was once again dismembered. All cinema is make-believe. The permanence we seek eludes us. But the essential point is clear enough, and comes over clearly in the film. Our past is our fortune. We exist as moral beings in so far as we possess, love and imitate ancestors.

This, anyway, is one side of the matter. But *The Mirror* is complicated art (how else could one justify the epithet 'great'?); and being complicated, touches other, sometimes contradictory moods. For the very weight of meaning which the past confers on the present elsewhere usurps individual freedom, and paralyses opportunity for action. That is another, more malign, aspect of mirror imagery. The mother and the wife of the narrator are played by the same actress, Margarita Terekhova. Yet we don't need Freud in order to enquire: should a man hanker after his

73

mother (or her image)? The narrator, it would appear, chooses his model of womanhood too faithfully, and his marriage breaks up as a consequence. Repetition, beyond a certain limit, is neurosis – is affliction. The film is replete with the possibility that the present is enchained to the past: modelled on it but somehow also cursed by it, leading to a history of forlorn, nervous, unsatisfied lives.

There are other things too, less easily definable, allusions that hover in and out of sight, in and out of hearing. Leonardo da Vinci is a certain point of reference. During the war the narrator, as a boy, discovers the beauty of art by leafing through a book containing illustrations of the great Italian's drawings – a scene pre-echoed in *Ivan's Childhood*. Although the famous mirror writing isn't dwelt upon (though viewers in the West might be tempted to think of the Cyrillic lettering that captions the illustrations as itself a form of 'mirror script'), the meditation which is set up in due course becomes curiously symmetrical. We could put it in words by asking, does Russia 'mirror' the West; or is it in fact part of the West? Those paintings by Leonardo: are they (from Tarkovsky's point of view) *his* tradition? Or are they necessarily the Other, the opposite, the speculum?

An answer to this is provided in some way later in the film, in the extract of the letter from Pushkin to Chaadayev which the boy Ignat reads aloud to the ghost-woman in his father's apartment. Chaadayev was an interesting figure, and worth a small parenthesis. A literary ex-guardsman with mystical tendencies, he travelled widely in Western Europe at the time of Nicholas I, before returning to Russia, convinced that the salvation and progress of his country depended on its conversion from Orthodoxy to Roman Catholicism. It was a dangerous view to preach at the time and the Emperor, it appears, had him entrusted to a physician. Pushkin, who knew Chaadayev well, wrote him a justly famous letter, parts of which are quoted by the boy. The letter's gist would appear to be this: the culture of Russia has its own proper quality, which looks to the West, but doesn't in any slavish way copy it. Far from being in debt to Europe, Russia had in fact relieved the West of the burden of fighting the Tartars, and thus established the conditions whereby Christianity could continue to flourish.

Now Pushkin himself was no earnest or evangelising Slavophile. (The letters to and from Chaadayev were, naturally, written in French.) The position which he outlined – Russia both in and out of Europe – can be seen, in its dignified precisions, as a patriotic middle way; the position of many educated Russians since, and

74

'A connection between present and past': flashback to a childhood incident

almost certainly the position of Tarkovsky. Holding up his country to the 'mirror' of the West, he allows certain truths to emerge, and become clarified. Yet what happens, Tarkovsky casually asks, if you turn it in a circuit of 180 degrees, and focus its gaze also on the East? Janus-faced Russia – the ancient grand dukedom of Muscovy – is poised also on the borders of Asia. In the newsreel sequences in the film Tarkovsky bounces his metaphor across the Urals, towards China. It is 1969, the time of disturbances on the Sino-Russian border (Damansky Island). Massed groups of Chinese, held back by struggling Soviet guards, surge towards the newsreel camera, waving in their hands the thoughts of Chairman Mao. Marxism, which issued out of Russia, seems to be directed back into it, with hostility. Does it belong there? Or is it (transformed by the Chinese into Maoism) an alien pestilence, a threat? Naturally the film can't say it is; but its transitions allow us to consider it a possibility. Nothing, perhaps, is more intellectually arresting in the film, or greater proof of Tarkovsky's independence.

Can we, then, come to a certainty about the symbol? There is a temptation to be too metaphysical. This chronicle of the filmmaker's family is also the story of other lives, of that whole generation which endured, under Stalinism, a collective fate. Tarkovsky opens his book *Sculpting in Time* by disputing the authorities' claim that his films are 'obscure' exercises in symbolism. On the contrary, he says, many people from all over the Soviet Union wrote to him about the truth of *The Mirror*; many people, then, saw their lives *mirrored* in his family's life – a 'typical' fate: not necessarily grand or important but lived through, suffered, and faithfully (he hopes) registered in memory.

The newsreel sequences
Besides the sequence just mentioned of the Chinese border disturbances, there are four other newsreel interventions. In the first of these, about halfway through the film, the reminiscences of a Spanish acquaintance of the narrator are interrupted by shots of the Civil War in Spain: specifically, the bombing of civilian populations (by Nationalist forces) and the panic that ensues from this, along with preparations for the evacuation of children.

Almost contiguous is another piece of newsreel footage with no seeming connection, showing the beginning of a record-breaking Russian balloon ascent on the stratosphere (1950s). The gondola is tethered to the ground, its massive dome rising above it; while smaller, one-man balloons, this time airborne, hover round its surface.

The third newsreel extract shows Soviet troops in the last war pushing their armoury across the shallows of Lake Sivash, in the Crimea. Connected to this, there is another rapid montage of shots showing, first, the liberation of Prague by the Red Army in 1945; next, a firework display in Moscow celebrating the end of the war; thirdly, the atom bomb exploding with eerie horror over Hiroshima.

What is the function of these episodes? As we have already seen, there is the fairly straightforward way in which they can be understood to broaden and generalise the personal, biographical experience to which the bulk of the film is given over. These episodes contextualise the sufferings of one particular family – the

76

narrator's. Belonging to ourselves, we belong also, irredeemably, to history. So much can be stated fairly easily. Yet nothing can prepare us for how genuinely extraordinary and beautiful these newsreels are in their own right. It is as if Tarkovsky were to find not only the relevant moment of history to coincide with his personal tale, but by some added touch of artistry to find it in a mode that has *already* been transformed into the richness and specificity of art.

Take the scenes from the Spanish Civil War. Bombs fall, as we have seen them fall in countless newsreels; houses explode, the civilian population scurries round in panic. Gradually the editing of the newsreel comes round to photographs of children at the evacuation points, crowded together with their pitiful suitcases, hugged by weeping relatives. The camera focuses on a little girl seated on her suitcase, long enough to register the moment when her charming smile changes into a frown of bewilderment. The whole film, it could be said, 'comes together' at this instant, the documentary truth of the child's pain seamlessly joining the fictional truth of the numerous other scenes of tenderness and suffering, in which the camera – Tarkovsky's own this time – lingers on the grave beauty of children.

The scenes on Lake Sivash should be mentioned in this context. Tarkovsky tells us in his book that he discovered them after much research. Quite a long time after finding the extracts he learnt that the cameraman responsible for filming them had been killed, along with most of the men who are pictured. We do not need this added poignancy to sense that the shots are exceptional – for the metaphysical sense of time unfolding at its own pace (not the pace of propaganda) as the men trudge, ankle-deep and weary, dragging their ordnance across the water. Such an episode is neither about defeat nor about victory. The overarching sky announces eternity, the water underneath has the placidity of dreams. Tarkovsky places the shots in the film without any explanation, and you feel any explanation would be impertinent. Their refulgence and beauty speak for themselves: speak for history, continuity, endeavour. The journey to Calvary is implicit; as also those numerous other potential journeys made by convicts in chains across the glittering Siberian wasteland. The sequence is as close as possible in Tarkovsky's work to absolute cinema. Nothing at all happens in it; everything is present or latent.

A world of wonder: the boy and his home

Love and memory

The cinema has not, in the past, been averse to experimenting with
time and memory. The classical films about memory – *Muriel,
Hiroshima mon amour, Citizen Kane, Vertigo, Letter From an
Unknown Woman* – shade off into the literally thousands of movies
which by using the device of the flashback set up some dramatic (or
ironic, or poignant) contrast between the past and the present. But
the depths of memory explored for their own sake and not as the
fulcrum of 'plot': that is definitely rarer. Memory must be
understood here in its purest form, as a mining of the deepest
recesses of childhood. Poetry and the novel have often worked in
this area, of course, but the cinema not nearly so extensively. One
of the central strengths of *The Mirror* lies in its simple power of
evocation: its ability to conjure up, in piercing epiphanies, that
magical submerged world of wonder which forms the adult's later
imaginative capital.

What truths, specifically, confront the child? The truths of shape and sensation: colour, sound, scent. And along with these, the primal affections: tenderness, love, fear, sorrow, rejection. *The Mirror*, not being a piece of psychological research, does not go into these things exhaustively. Its mode of evocation is the mode of art; that is, the mode of allusion. Thus the experiences it describes are necessarily, in one sense, particular. But at a certain stage in all interesting art the particular moves over into the universal. This is what I think happens in *The Mirror*.

There is first that discovery of colour. In the earliest memories of the film, the boy is perhaps three or four years old. Cries of alarm come from the direction of the neighbour's house. 'Dunya.' 'What is it, Pasha?' 'A fire!' Outside, in the clearing, the stout wooden building is already ablaze. Instead of running to the rescue, adults and children stand transfixed, amazed by its transfiguring beauty. Tarkovsky comes back here, as again and again, to his feeling that among the deepest moments of childhood are those spent aimlessly (yet not so aimlessly after all) at the side of the brazier or the domestic hearth, watching the flames lick and curl round the embers; orange at one moment and at the next vermilion, turquoise, emerald, deepest blue.

Meanwhile, in the same scene, the unused bucket clanks against the side of the well: one of those peaceful, monotonous noises of childhood that are stored away at the back of our memories. To which Tarkovsky adds at different points in the film the creaking of a hammock under the bough, the clanging of a gate-latch in the wind, the summer susurration of grass, the tapestry of birdcall, the faraway whistle of a train, all carefully interwoven with modern and classical music.*

Such aural notations are finely marked in and make an indispensable contribution to the film's subliminal richness.† Above all,

---

*A film by the Russian animator Yuri Norstein, *Tale of Tales* (1979; surely one of the most lovely cartoons ever filmed), seems to offer a number of similarities, most notably in its soundtrack. In a film about childhood memory one remembers the opening: the sight of a baby sucking at its mother's breast, sounds of the mother's heart. Later, apples roll in an earthenware jar; a bonfire crackles, on which the protagonist (a little wolf) is seen roasting potatoes. Picking them too hot from the blaze the little wolf blows on their surface to cool them, juggles them from paw to paw. Cars whoosh by on the nearby motorway as he tucks into his solitary night-time picnic. There is an extraordinary sense of melancholy poetry.

†Jean-Pierre Jeancolas has written an excellent essay on *The Mirror*'s soundtrack in *Positif*, no. 206, May 1978.

however, there is a wonderful feeling for space. 'Space' here is perhaps not easy to define. Many families (who needs reminding?) have no space at all. A phenomenology of its own attaches to being reared in a city apartment block. Tarkovsky's childhood was privileged in the sense that it was experienced in the country. The simple peasant mansion of his parents was 'complicated' enough to have a surplus of vistas and corridors and secret spaces, rooms that led off into other rooms, attics, cupboards and outhouses. These are all beautifully present in the film: you feel them with the child's quiet wonder. The wood from the forest provides the planks for the floors and the half-timbering of the outside walls. We can almost smell the polish on the old dressers. Wild meadow flowers are placed in vases and jars on the window-sills. Lace curtains flap in the breeze, the bed-linen flaps on the washing-line – a hundred shapes for a child's imagination (the topmost mast of a galleon, a

Waiting: Margarita Terekhova

whispering convocation of ghosts). The mother's love for her children presides over all this, shapes it into order and friendliness. Truly it is remarked that one *learns* happiness in the fortunes of childhood. If it is never experienced then, it may never be experienced subsequently.

Anxiety

All happiness has an element of anxiety, inseparable from the fear of the source being taken away. There are the separations in the film caused by war; and other separations, temporary perhaps but no less painful, caused by unspecified marital difficulties. Informing *The Mirror*'s flashback scenes at every level is the great Russian wartime emotion of waiting: the woman's longing for the return of her husband, so beautifully summarised (with its not-to-be-played-down ingredient of boredom and bitterness: 'You can't smooth things away with a tear, or wipe them away with a handkerchief') in the opening scene of Margarita Terekhova on the fence looking pensively out over the wheatfield.

There are also reunions. These include the wife and children on necessarily different levels. Two brief cameos capture the emotions classically connected with such events, in their familial and sexual resonance. In the first, the very young child wakes up in the night with the word 'Papa' on his lips. Creeping out of bed, he looks through the door of his room. A robe flies by, thrown by his father. Night-time and love. The child is excluded. But in the other, later scene – possibly a parting, possibly a reunion – it is day-time, and the uniformed father clasps his children to his body in a gesture of tender solicitude.

Other memories include the memory of pity (the origin of the child's moral life). A central scene takes us to a rifle range in winter-time where a party of children, including the narrator as a twelve-year-old boy, is being instructed in elementary shooting-drill. There is bitter cold weather and snow on the ground. A small child named Asafyev proves refractory. Given the command to 'about turn', he insists for some reason on wheeling a full 360 degrees. The instructor repeats his order, but the boy stubbornly repeats the manoeuvre. Tears trickle down his face. The instructor questions him, threatening to report him to his parents. Yet the parents are dead (so the other children gleefully inform the instructor).

The sequel to this episode follows immediately. While the boys pass up the bank, little Asafyev, as if by some pre-arranged wager,

81

takes hold of a hand-grenade and releases the pin, rolling the bomb down on to the rifle range. The instructor catches sight of what is happening, and throws his body, without hesitating, as a shield between the grenade and his students. Silence and suspense. The thumps of the man's heart are magnified on the soundtrack. As the camera slowly wheels round to capture his face, one notices that beneath his fallen helmet a shaven patch on his skull, the size of an egg, is visibly contracting and expanding, in furious time to the rhythm of his heart.

The scene is shot with extraordinary clarity and deftness, the detail of the skull-beat adding that indefinable authenticity, indication of Tarkovsky's perfectionism. The scene's power, however, lies in Tarkovsky's human understanding of the boy's and the instructor's extraordinary sadness, the odd, unspoken collusion between the two. (All is well: the bomb is only a practice grenade.) There is a chastening moment, captured here, in all of our lives when we first really encounter someone else's loneliness.

Speech

In the debates about philosophy and literature that have taken place in the West over the last fifteen years or so there has emerged a tendency to deny the relation between speech and authenticity. Language, it has been remarked, speaks us (rather than the other way round). The self is a fiction, an impossible metaphysical entity. In the general trawl of ideologies (going with a concomitant decline in religious faith) an extreme scepticism has grown up about whether language can ever find, or master, truth. This is experienced explicitly, for example, in the films of Jean-Luc Godard, with their multifarious, ironical 'texts' banging up against each other, quarrelling and dissolving. But it is an assumption which, on a general level, has moved into academic discourse; and in fact the condition of Modernism – or post-Modernism – is informed by it.

The specific philosophical arguments for and against this position are, by their nature, complicated; and, plainly, on an intuitive level the artist is not concerned with them. All one can say is that Tarkovsky, in his belief in the *necessary connection* between language and truth, stands at the opposite pole to a modernist like Godard. This comes out fairly unambiguously in *The Mirror*, particularly in the marvellous pre-credits sequence, showing a session of hypnosis during which a boy becomes cured of his stutter. We see the boy at first painfully attempting to articulate his name. Then the woman doctor, brisk and authoritative, puts him into hypnosis, and proceeds to draw his tension out, first from the back of his head, then from his hands. 'I'll count to three and your hands will go rigid,' she says. 'I'll remove this condition and you can speak. Loudly and clearly, freely and easily, unafraid of your voice. As you speak now, you will speak for the rest of your life. Say, when I count to three, loudly and clearly, "Now I can speak!"'

'Now I can speak!' And the boy does speak out, clearly, articulately. The sequence was apparently set up by Tarkovsky with a real stammerer and a real doctor. (We don't see it because Tarkovsky cuts, but the film crew was stunned by the experience, some of them weeping.) The power of the word combined with its ability to define truth is almost, perhaps, the single central article of faith that Tarkovsky is testifying to in *The Mirror*. We sense it, again, in the use of his father's poetry (spoken by Arseny himself) at certain key moments of recollection, as the camera, following its own path, explores the recesses of the house and its environment. What is to be said about these poems? Two things perhaps: first, how genuinely eloquent they are, in a way that surprises us in the West who have become inured over the years to the general decline of poetic currency. For modern Western poetry, with popular exceptions, is no longer a truly *spoken* form, its power, if there is any, being transmissible solely via the printed page. In the modulations of Arseny Tarkovsky's lines, however, one feels the excitement of oral poetry, as it must have existed back in the time of Pushkin. For it seems that the tradition of the voice (which in the West has moved over into song) has never really died in the Soviet Union – a fact we know to be true from the evidence of the great prison memoirists: Ginzburg, Solzhenitsyn, Kopelev, Von Meck etc. Memorised metrical speech as a spiritual pabulum that could not be taken away from you by anyone appears to have played, in both the 19th and 20th centuries, an extraordinarily important role in the life of the camps.*

*Let us include Edmund Wilson's testimony as a visitor to the country in the period of its darkest uncertainty: 'One might perhaps see a revival of verse in a period and in a society in which music played a leading role in general serious culture. This has long been the case in Russia; and in Russia at the present time people declaim poetry at drinking parties and while travelling on railroad trains almost as readily as they sing. They go to poetry readings as we go to concerts. It is probable that, at the present time, the Russians care more about poetry than any other European people. Their language, strongly accented and half sung, lends itself peculiarly to verse.' *The Triple Thinkers* (1938), p. 39.

The second thing to note is that these poems are so simple. They exist not so much in ambiguity as in statement. 'The table is the same for the grandfather and the grandson.' When, I wonder, did we in the West last have a poetry like this, which took responsibility for experience, instead of ironising it out of existence? In an interview conducted in 1966 soon after the completion of *Andrei Roublev*, Tarkovsky referred to Pushkin's *The Prophet* (1822) as 'summarising' his views about art. The narrator, in the midst of spiritual travails ('athirst in gloom'), meets a strange six-winged seraph on the road, who 'laid his finger on my eyes'.

> And the wise serpent's tongue he placed
> Between my lips with hand blood-dabbled;
> And with a sword he clove my breast,
> Plucked out the heart he made beat higher,
> And in my stricken bosom pressed.
> Instead of coal, a living fire!
>
> Upon the waste, a lifeless clod,
> I lay, and heard the word of God:
> 'Arise, O prophet, watch and hearken,
> And with my will thy soul engird,
> Roam the grey seas, the roads that darken,
> And burn men's hearts with this, my Word.'
> (Translation: Babette Deutsch)

Can the 'Word' ever again speak with such confidence? This is the serious question of *The Mirror*. The tone of Arseny's poems is, like Pushkin's, that of thrilling, lofty affirmation:

> On earth there is no death.
> All are immortal. All is immortal. No need
> To be afraid of death at seventeen
> Nor yet at seventy. Reality and light
> Exist, but neither death nor darkness.
> All of us are on the sea-shore now,
> And I am one of those who haul the nets
> When a shoal of immortality comes in.

('One of those who haul the nets / When a shoal of immortality comes in': it is a splendid definition of the poet and film-maker. The poem goes on):

84

Live in the house – and the house will stand.
I will call up any century,
Go into it and build myself a house.
That is why your children are beside me
And your wives, all seated at one table,
One table for great-grandfather and grandson.
The future is accomplished here and now,
And if I slightly raise my hand before you
You will be left with all five beams of light.
With shoulder blades like timber props
I held up every day that made the past,
With a surveyor's chain I measured time
And travelled through as if across the Urals.

(Translation: Kitty Hunter Blair)

The poet here, we can see, is a sort of Promethean figure, an Atlas: blessing, memorialising and upholding. In speaking thus, the Tarkovskys (father and son) speak for those who are 'unable to speak'. But the gift of prophecy is not, in turn, their own property: rather, it is lent from outside, from 'above'. This aspiration, or inspiration (the 'breath of God'), is dramatised at key moments of the film by a perceptible objective correlative: a kind of rustling of the wind, or susurration. We see it first in the scene at the beginning of the film where the stranger (Anatoly Solonitsin), having met Margarita Terekhova at the gate, walks back across the field to the pathway. Before he gets there a mysterious gust of wind rushes out of nowhere, converting the landscape into a swaying sea of wheat. He turns, bemused, and the same thing happens. There is no 'logical' explanation for the phenomenon (for the sky is clear). It is a moment of pure grace and mystery.

Right at the end of the film, too, on a long travelling shot, the wind once again blows up, this time from thè depths of the forest. Now the camera backs away into the forest for the final shot of the film, suggesting a quality of agency. A 'partnership' is set up between the force of God (or nature) and the force of the poet (or film-maker); a partnership which would be blasphemous and absurd if the film itself, by its gravity and tactfulness, had not managed, in all its other shots, splendidly to validate it.

Actors
The discussion may have inadvertently given the impression that *The Mirror* does not have any people in it, at least people one cares

85

about and likes. But I do not think this is true. As the fence collapses on which he has seated himself beside the rather sulky Terekhova, the stranger jokes: 'It is always pleasant to fall with an interesting woman!' Tarkovsky possesses the somewhat difficult-to-describe power (plainly, however, a film-maker's *sine qua non*) of making all his characters three-dimensional. This grave and exalted film is at certain moments very witty. There is the flashback scene when the mother, fearing she has made a terrible mistake in the state printing house where she works, tears back to check up on the proofs. The sense of universal relief when it turns out to be a false alarm is wonderfully conveyed by the actress.* The whole brave sequence is memorable: Terekhova's marvellous stride as she flies down the corridor, all heartbeat and recklessness (she half mocks the mistake that may ruin her); the elegant friend Elisaveta (Alla Demidova) who accuses her of giving herself the airs of a character out of Dostoevsky ('Anyway, who *is* Maria Timofeyevna?'†); the hysterical new employee (female) who fears that their carelessness will send them all off to a labour camp; finally, the willowy male colleague who can be trusted (Nikolai Grinko), settling the episode with a comforting libation of vodka (glasses are handy in the filing cabinet). We experience unportentously a brief moment of life under Stalinism in all its brittle and dangerous gaiety. The characters have freedom and irony. Also, when appropriate, elegance. They resist being summed up by the system.

The modern scenes too (Terekhova as wife rather than mother) have sufficient richness of characterisation: a sense of explanations held back; proper reticences in keeping with the fact that the director is dramatising proud, wayward human beings, and that life, after all, is quite complicated. Thus, for example, the specific reasons for the marriage between the narrator and his wife breaking down are not anatomised; but you gather all you need to know (including the degree to which either party still loves the other) from the sharpness and economy of one or two unambiguous dialogues. The same goes for the backwardness (or rather, awkwardness) of the boy Ignat. It is not because I think such episodes unimportant, rather because in a certain sense they speak

---

*It emerges that Stalin's name is phonetically similar to the Russian verb meaning to shit: 'Shralin'. Maria, no prude, whispers it into her confidante's ear.

†Lebyatkin's (bossy) sister in *The Devils*. 'When you dislike something you simply wrinkle up your nose at it.'

False alarm at the state printing house (Nikolai Grinko, Alla Demidova, Margarita Terekhova)

for themselves, that I have held back from going into them exhaustively. But they are there as part of the film's overall humanity.

Cubism

The Mirror has been described as a mosaic. As you move round inside it and over it, different facets – different clusters of tessera – catch the light and gleam momentarily. Another metaphor, more homely, is the peasant patchwork quilt. Still another comparison is with Cubist painting, which seeks to include on the two-dimensional plane all the angles and contours that are usually only encountered in sculpture.

Such, at least, is the habitual description of Cubism's function. But I wonder if I am alone in finding a gap between what apologists say Cubism is, and what is actually experienced on the canvas. Is Cubism 'theatre-in-the-round'? Or is it irrevocably abstract? The claims that have been made for this experiment in painting have been very high indeed, as one notes in books on the subject by influential writers like Edward Fry, John Berger and John Golding.* But it has always seemed to me that the problem of Cubism is whether it possesses spiritual 'content'. Does it, at the simplest level, tell us anything about life that we did not know before? Does it succeed in placing what one does know in new and artistic conjunctions?

The cinema, I would want to say, is now a far greater art form than painting. Painting did not give up its supremacy overnight, and indeed in certain areas still has not done so. The 'childishness' of cinema, which must have been so evident in 1910 when Braque and Picasso were experimenting, is still of course prevalent today (as a visit to the West End of any great city makes obvious). Nonetheless, it does seem to me that a film like *The Mirror* really *answers* Cubism. What I mean is that it looks at its subject *from all angles*; and more than this, it has something substantial and intelligent to look at. There is so much that modern art does not cover, or covers too obliquely to turn it into a discourse of common language. History, the countryside, the passions of adult men and women, the faces of God and the angels, the meaning of fire, earth, water. Is that putting it unfairly? Cubism, we are told, has its marvellous still lifes. But so has *The Mirror*, I find myself answering, and so have all Tarkovsky's other films. There is the milk on the table, the bread and utensils; all freshly seen, great and intelligible.

Flight

Flying is one of the great motifs of traditional painting. The urge to depict winged seraphim as a deep and noble impulse seems to have survived long after the vanishing of a literal belief in the existence of angels. In Max Ernst and the painters of surrealism this urge is sardonic and ghostly; in Chagall and the peasant tradition it is naive and nostalgic. We wonder whether the nineteenth-century artist Delacroix believed in the sublime angels and winged figures with which he decorated the walls of Saint Sulpice. Tarkovsky, at any event, follows in the great painterly tradition in his serious depiction of such wonders. The images of floating women in his work (Hari in *Solaris*, the Icelandic woman in *The Sacrifice*, as well

*Respectively, *Cubism* (London, 1966), *The Moment of Cubism and Other Essays* (London, 1969) and *Cubism: A History and Analysis* (revised edition 1987). I am thinking also of the essays on Picasso in Leo Steinberg's *Other Criteria* (New York, 1972).

88

The levitation of Maria

as Maria here) return us to the oldest and deepest urges in art: to the ecstasy of finding that not only is the earth peopled, but also the air and the heavens.

Other film memoirs of Stalinism

The genre is rare, but will probably become less so, particularly after the pioneering fantastical exposé of Beria's police methods in Tengiz Abuladze's *Repentance* (1986). Another film which revolves round the police in the 1930s, and combines with this a private meditation on the family, is Alexei Guęrman's *My Friend Ivan Lapshin* (1984). The director (son of the distinguished 1950s short story writer and film scenarist Yuri Guerman) has two previous films to his credit – one of which, *Roadcheck* (1971), a sympathetic account of a Second World War deserter, ran into similar trouble as *The Mirror*.

My Friend Ivan Lapshin is an interesting work, though quite different in tone from *The Mirror*. (Tarkovsky spoke admiringly of Guerman in interviews. Whether this admiration was for his technique, or his content, or a combination of the two, I remain uncertain.) The film, quasi-autobiographical, centres on the friendship that develops because of shared living accommodation between the narrator's parents and the local police detective (criminal police, not NKVD), a handsome maverick figure, strict and successful but somewhat bohemian in the conduct of his private life. Shot in period black and white, it manages to capture with extraordinary precision and particularity the actual texture of the 1930s, rather as Tarkovsky does in the printing house scene in *The Mirror*. We see the shabbiness of the buildings, the threadbare clothes, the makeshift transport and living quarters. We feel the cold in winter. But the film also dramatises a sort of frenetic gaiety in the midst of all this – an atmosphere conducive to serious thoughts, and to love affairs.

Where the film differs from *The Mirror* is in concerning itself with a strictly communist milieu. The characters are all in some sense Party believers. The film wants to ask: what was believed communism like in the 1930s? Was it *right* to be communist? The verdict is unclear; for if the director sees the socialist experiment as melancholy, he still does not really see it as mistaken. There is a sort of materialist brutality underpinning the characters' romanticism, leaving the spiritual content of the film distant from *The Mirror*'s tender religious humanism.

Ivan Lapshin in turn, however, reminds one of a Yugoslav film of roughly similar date and impact, Emir Kusturica's *Father is Away on Business* (1985 Cannes prize-winner). The two films are united in their portrayal of intelligent, dangerous and rather attractive protagonists whose political allegiance remains obstinately Stalinist. Kusturica's film, as the title implies, does not deliberately tackle this head-on: the hero is absent, for at least some of the time, in jail (Yugoslavia, 1948: Stalinism is imprisonable). As in *Ivan Lapshin*, it is the child's view of the epoch which dominates. Both films ask, from their slightly different generational viewpoints, before and after the war: what was it like to have grown up in the era of totalitarianism? The honesty of both answers is impressive. Kusturica, no less than Guerman, wishes to say that in a curious way (as in all childhoods) it was happy.

Such films raise, perhaps, the issue of whether cinema is ever capable of saying all the things that should be said and must be said; whether it possesses, in particular, the generalising power of literature which would allow us to see not only the incident, but the incident in its moral-historical resonance. Does there exist a cinematic equivalent (to stay with Yugoslavia for the moment) to the great central memoirs of Milovan Djilas, where – with a poet's scorn and a historian's fine objectivity – Stalinism is definitively 'anatomised'. And, by extension, is the power of Tarkovsky in these matters comparable to the power of a Solzhenitsyn?

The argument seems to divide up between those critics who say that cinema does indeed find an adequate truth; those who say that *some* truth is better than none; and a third faction which has it that anything less than the whole truth is an apology, if not a betrayal. Can films like *Ivan Lapshin* and *Father is Away on Business* really be seen as 'revisionist' and 'objectively' on the side of the authorities? A sensible person would be inclined to think not. And this extends to powerful films like *Man of Marble* (Andrzej Wajda, Poland, 1976), *A Diary* (Márta Mészáros, Hungary, 1984), *Another Way* (Károly Makk, Hungary, 1981) and *Angi Vera* (Pál Gábor, Hungary, 1978) – films which open up investigations into the moral history of communism that are fundamental, and henceforward unignorable. In the works just cited, as in *The Mirror*, it is no longer even a question of 'reading between the lines'. A scoundrel is a scoundrel anywhere, and these films say so. Likewise, the conditions that attach to good and noble behaviour are more universal than many people think.

STALKER

Stalker is the account of a journey by two men and their guide through a mysteriously unspecified zone full of invisible dangers. The object of the journey is obscure, for even though the men arrive at their destination – a tumble-down house with a water-filled inner chamber – and manage to make the return crossing, it is not clear whether the trip has been a success. Indeed it seems not to have been, except from the guide's point of view, since his crippled daughter is cured (or perhaps she is). The guide is known only by his nickname, Stalker; the two travellers are Writer and Scientist. Plainly we are in the presence of allegory. And it might be thought that the most profitable discussion of the film would be strictly interpretative.

To a certain extent this is true. And yet the discussion of art that is solely hermeneutic carries with it its own distortions. A critic can over-explain a work of art, and in doing so betray the experience. Why are certain films instinctively sensed as serious and good? The reasons are multifarious, and don't necessarily have to do with their philosophy. This, paradoxically, is why there is room in the world for formalist criticism (the kind of criticism, for instance, which examines a film from the point of view of its editing procedures), since the essential beauty of the work concerned – hence its grandeur, importance and authority – may indeed be formal, or quasi-formal.

Pure formalism in critical writing, I think, is never wholly satisfactory, but one sometimes feels one knows what it is driving at. When, for instance, I look at a film like Dreyer's *Gertrud* (1964), it is not its description of love that moves me (in certain ways I disagree with it). What arrests me is the film's boldness as cinema, the patient way in which the camera moves across the human form, converting it into living monumental sculpture. The purity that is expressed is as hard to define as the purity of music. And as with music the film seems to possess its own secret morality, parallel to, but different from, the explicit one.

This is rather what I feel about *Stalker*. Its pleasure is firstly a pure pleasure of film. Certain things happen in the story, and plainly they have to be commented on; but the travelling towards those incidents, and between them, contains its own private mysterious wonders. Tarkovsky said that he would like to have left the impression that his film was shot in a single continuous take; and, taking him at his word, one can agree that on one level the film is indeed as experimental as any work of the non-commercial avant-garde. Like the avant-garde artists (Frampton, Snow, Le Grice etc.), the director examines the meaning of time within the scope of a series of extended sequence shots. He appears to be interested in bringing into the protocols of narrative art something of the experience (the rhythms, the patience, even the boredom) of real experienced human time and anguish.

We can see this most clearly in the long and celebrated sequence of the trolley ride that takes the men from their hiding place on the far side of the border up to the edges of the Zone, whence they are to continue on foot. The camera is mounted on a railcar. There is no dialogue for approximately three minutes (a long time in cinema terms). The only sound is the clanking of the wheels over the sleepers, as we watch the tense serious faces of the men against a background of passing foliage and landscape. Why isn't the scene boring if nothing at all happens in it? Now, the pure avant-garde often *is* dull (it is part of its complicated puritanism). But I doubt whether such provocations were Tarkovsky's intention here. The scene, paradoxically, is full of human interest. Tarkovsky, you could say, takes his time, almost uniquely in modern cinema, to look at men's faces inquisitively. His gaze is not of the type that we call psychological but something older, more strictly related to sculpture and painting. The shaven heads of Stalker and his companions take us back to certain great moments in silent cinema: to Falconetti, perhaps, in Dreyer's *Passion of Joan of Arc*, or to the nude sculpted heads (so lovingly dwelt upon and circled round) of the peasant convocation in Dovzhenko's *Earth*.

Actually *Earth* provides in more ways than one an instance of my general argument. On the narrative level it is scarcely coherent, being completely confused as to whether it is supporting, or attacking, the infamous collectivisation of the peasantry. The film's intense beauty and integrity are to be grasped, on the other hand, in certain moments of transition: *temps morts*, glimpses of the sky and the landscape as they have never been photographed before; chance collocations of gesture, and expressions of mysterious rapt nobility.

Stalker: the trolley leaves for the Zone

In *Stalker* the sequence of the trolley lasts long enough to bring in these metaphysical reflections; yet not so long as to abandon narrative altogether. This is an extremely delicate balancing act, reproduced every time the camera slides off into one of its astonishingly controlled, seemingly endless travelling shots – shots which interrogate nature (earth, moss, bushes, streams, ruins) with an intensity and a duration that has seldom been equalled. A few extra seconds on either side and the exercise would be 'merely' avant-garde, in the derogatory sense. Instead, the shots flow with classical rightness. Tarkovsky teaches us (what classical artists have always understood) that economy of means issues in freedom rather than in constriction. Thus, if the film's tone is pessimistic – at least, reined in and low-key – its imagery, and its harmonies, are extraordinarily grave and resplendent.*

*The film was shot twice over, a very rare occurrence in commercial cinema (Ophuls' *Letter From an Unknown Woman* is the only other example I can think of), owing to a processing fault at the laboratories which ruined the negative. One thinks of the dedication involved in picking up the pieces, starting anew, and making it even *better* the second time around.

Who or what is the Stalker?

The above remarks may seem to prevaricate, but it is not my intention to evade an analysis of the film's content. The film enacts a parable which demands an effort of elucidation in good faith. The clue to its meaning resides in the tale of Porcupine which, sometime in the course of the journey, emerges in the men's collective reminiscence.

Porcupine, apparently, was a previous guide to the Zone who became accidentally responsible for his brother's death. Wishing to repent, he set out into the Zone to find the Secret Place where his prayer might be granted, and the brother be brought back to life. Locating the Room (a secular equivalent, it seems, to the Chapel of the Holy Grail), he prayed and returned: only to discover that not this, but a more private, clandestine wish had been granted, and that he had become on the spot immensely wealthy. When he emerged from the Zone his remorse returned with redoubled intensity, and we learn that he hanged himself.

A moral tale, evidently. Transferring the parable-within-a-parable to the fortunes of the three men on screen, we arrive at a schema like the following: the Writer and the Scientist, men of reason and language, journey to the edge of possibility but are unable to make the final crossing. They are unable to find within themselves the profound humility which makes faith bountiful. In a way their articulacy itself holds them back, just as their expertise renders them ineffectual. In short, they can't, at bottom, summon up the life-and-death sincerity which converts desire into fruition. In the case of Stalker, by contrast, humility of soul is untainted by worldliness. His heart is empty of egotism. He is the 'weak' man, the uninsistent one, the pilgrim. For this reason alone it becomes possible for his prayers to be granted.

'Possible': it is not clear, as I say, whether they *are* granted. The final sequences contain a visual *glissade*, for just as we see that the Stalker's crippled daughter Monkey is walking for the first time, the camera pulls back, revealing the girl being carried on her father's shoulders. Nonetheless wonders – 'benedictions' – are in the air. *Stalker* introduces a number of quasi-religious ideas that become vital in Tarkovsky's later work, concerning the necessity of religious belief and miracles.

There is no need to stress at the outset how distant such a view of life is from that of most contemporary artistic discourse. For if one regards the supernatural a jot less sympathetically than Tarkovsky and his protagonists do (and a jot here makes all the difference since, it could be argued, either one 'believes' or one does not), the whole of his drama, and with it a great part of his claims as a film-maker, dissolves into a bundle of gesture.

Before trying to respond to this rather acute difficulty, I ought perhaps to set it out more clearly. Let me start with this generalisation: in fiction and drama we in the West have tended in the past to measure morality by action. A protagonist behaves in certain ways in relation to his family, his country and his enemies. Starting from adversity, he moves to overcome his fears, and in the responsible choice for his actions the reader (or the audience) will measure his character. So, at least, in conventional realist fiction as we know it from the great classic novels and the most famous narrative films. But in 'late' Tarkovsky we are met with something that can only be described as an elevation of powerlessness, a hostility to conventional action, a quietism. The state of affairs seems to be connected to the current world crisis. Tarkovsky says: We live under a nuclear threat, brought about, partly, by the false allegiance to reason and action of men like the Scientist and the Writer. Only a complete inner change of heart by each and every one of us – a personal conversion and re-submission to God's will – can grasp the extent of the peril, and work for its eventual defusion.

It is a serious enough theme, fit for the statesman and the churchman. As a film-maker, Tarkovsky's artistic problem is to find a statement of belief that is sufficiently clear within a text that is sufficiently complex. For the purpose of art is not to propose solutions, but to set problems in their requisite depth. For this reason, elucidation of films like *Stalker* and, later, *The Sacrifice* becomes inherently awkward, since their spiritual authenticity, their value as searchingness, is so much bound up with a deliberate unresolvable perplexity. They both want and don't want to be 'explicated'. In this case there is a further, related problem. The character of Stalker, which the film suggests to be good, comes over as timorous and vacillating.

'What is weak is good: hardness is closest to death.' (Alternatively: 'Hardness and strength are Death's companions.') The line in the film from Arseny Tarkovsky's poem states the difficulty as clearly as it needs to be stated. The word 'weak' appears to be deployed with a special meaning attached to it – the meaning, perhaps, that we find in Dostoevsky rather than in Chekhov. Chekhov's plays are full of ineffectual characters whose feebleness needs no further comment. The playwright tolerates them, as he magnificently tolerates all his creations, at the same time as judging

96

As though he were a landscape': Alexander Kaidanovsky as the haven-headed Stalker

them clear-sightedly. Whereas the radicalness of a novel like *The Idiot* (and of Dostoevsky in general) is that it proposes the hero Myshkin's feebleness as another guise for spiritual resourcefulness. Weakness *is* strength in Dostoevsky – a contradiction not, after all, paradoxical to Christians.

Stated in another way, then, Tarkovsky's wish in the film seems to be to find for the Stalker the filmic equivalent of the 'spiritual' ambiguity of a Prince Myshkin. Does he succeed? Myshkin is earnest and eloquent: but the cinema (when it is understood properly) is a quasi-silent medium. As in painting, the important truths have to be conveyed through gesture. Tarkovsky commands the camera to look at Kaidanovsky (Stalker) not as though he were

97

an actor declaiming portentous lines, but as though he were, somehow, a landscape: unique, weathered, sculpted and natural. His shaven head suggests suffering, without composing that suffering into a gesture of pathos. Stalker's vulnerability, in short, resists being pinned down. Is he a peasant or a prince? He is muscular, but at the same time 'neurotic'; masculine, but with feminine characteristics. In sum, he is opaque and ungraspable.

Miracles
I have put these observations in terms of a problem about the film, but perhaps, after all, it is not quite so difficult. Stalker, like any interesting fictional protagonist (since we are speaking of Dostoevsky, we might add Aloysha from *The Brothers Karamazov*), has two conflicting sides to his personality. We see his fear – sense it, rather, acutely – in the scene before going into the Zone, where the men are sitting crouched in the landrover waiting for the moment to make a dash to the border. Time and again Kaidanovsky's features, the whole posture of his body, seem to be wracked by perplexity: more than this, by self-pity. (For example, the scene where he wrestles feebly with Scientist at the Threshhold; or later, returned from the journey, lying on the floor, groaning to his wife: 'My God I'm tired. *If you only knew how tired I was.*')

But against this, there are numerous instances making up, really, the body of the film where you sense in an unambiguous way his spiritual calmness and authority. Such sequences would include the quiet moment when he peers down the well-shaft and voices, inaudibly to his companions, the noble prayer about the ravages of will that is based on another poem by Tarkovsky's father. Or again, there is the central sequence of the film, the period of rest and dream by the side of the brook. Here we hear extracts from the Apocalypse and from the disciples' journey to Emmaus (Luke 24:13, the appearance before them of the risen Christ). The foetally curled body of Stalker (guarded by an Anubian Alsatian) emanates a wonderful serenity. Stalker awakes, and addresses to his still quarrelling travelling companions brief healing words about music, which despatch in an instant the slowly built-up burden of anguish.

All this allows us to surmise that the actual existence of the supernatural is not in the event quite so crucial. If Tarkovsky is friendly to the idea of religion and miracles (and the whole film demonstrates it), the ethical significance of life is still to be found in the concrete ordeals of experience. Love itself is the miracle, we could say; as the tender closing sequence of the film confirms, when we see Stalker back in the border town with his wife and child (walking or not, we don't know), the dog lapping the milk, the train rumbling past on the tracks, a love poem (in a woman's voice) being recited – poverty of circumstance but the deepest communion of spirit.

Writer and Scientist
Writer and Scientist, of course, are foils to Stalker, interestingly enough differentiated. Their spiritual torment seems to stop just short of faith (Tarkovsky in this film wants to show faith's *difficulty*). Writer, in the sly, excellent performance of Anatoly Solonitsin, is one of those cynical Russians we have often come across: a drinker, a wit, a man without metaphysical illusions ('No Gods, no goblins, no Bermuda Triangle'). His hopelessness from

Stalker in the Zone

99

the point of view of salvation is mitigated by the fact that he does actually wish to visit the Zone; and not just for touristic reasons either, or as a seeker after inspiration for his novels. Writer's profundity (if we can use the word in this context) lies in his instinctive hatred of the rationalist position – the idea that all explanations are ultimately materialist – summed up by his numerous witty jibes against Scientist.

Scientist (the rangy Nikolai Grinko, looking at times remarkably like the physicist Yuri Sakharov) is, for his part, equally enigmatic. He holds his cards to his chest: what his ambitions are in visiting the Zone only properly emerge, by action, at the climax of the journey, when he produces from his rucksack a pocket nuclear device and prepares to blow the Room to smithereens. Scientist, then, is the anti-Faustian man, whose proposed course of action aligns him with his mythical medieval adversary. His logical argument would seem to run like this: the Room is a danger to mankind, because in its mere existence lies the possibility of a future exploitation at the hands of unscrupulous tyrants. Rid the world of it now, and we rid the world of a false ideal, a Utopia. My blackmail, he says, is 'compassionate': I want a lesser hurt now, to avoid a bigger hurt later.

Naturally, Scientist completely misunderstands the metaphysical and private nature of the Room. Writer understands it but fails, when the moment of testing comes, to trust his soul to the Room's terrible scrutiny. Tarkovsky makes their differences clear enough psychologically, but at the same time doesn't, I think, overallegorise their opposition. They are human beings rather than mere intellectual ciphers. At different times each of the men – Stalker, Writer and Scientist – speaks and behaves with an unforeseen authority over the other two.

What and where is the Zone?

In the novel which the film was based on, *Roadside Picnic* by the Strugatsky brothers (1975), the 'Zones' (there are more than one) have been caused by the incursion of aliens who thirty years previously had paused at six points on the Earth's surface, 'picnicked' and gone off again, leaving behind them a trail of radio-active debris. Inside the areas where they landed there is a time-warp. Nothing has been altered or built over. The terrain is dangerous but, from the point of view of scientific research, valuable. Men like Stalker make a rough, alcoholic living as guides to the visiting scientists.

Tarkovsky cuts down, as film-makers have to, on the detail. The world he builds up is a physical one, different from, though based upon, the novelists' outline. Various strands of imagery seem to lie on top of each other like a palimpsest. If I tentatively dismantle these for the purposes of discussion, it ought to be with the understanding that none is more privileged than the other. All work together, polyphonically, to lend the film its complexity and depth.

The drama opens with an extended shot through the bedroom door of Stalker's billet, outside the Zone. Stalker is asleep in bed with his wife and child. An aerial shot moves across the bed and back again, as the vibration of a passing freight train rattles a glass of water on the bedside chair. Stalker wakes and rises quietly, passing into the front room to wash. Seconds later his wife (Alissa Freindlikh) follows him, and questions him about his planned journey. She is unable to prevent him from leaving and gives way, once he has gone, to a frenzied outburst of grief.*

Immediately noticeable in this scene are the surroundings: the shared bed, the bare walls, the anonymous drab clothing. One senses, in the intolerable strain of parting placed upon conjugal happiness, an image out of the 1930s and 40s. More than this: Stalker, with his shaved head and quasi-convict gear (we learn that he has been in jail previously) is the image of one of Solzhenitsyn's 'Zeks'. Russia itself in these images is the prison camp, the land of sorrows. (Lev Kopelev, in his excellent prison memoir *No Jail for Thought*, 1977, reminds us that the Gulag area in the Soviet Union was known to its inhabitants as 'The Zone'.) There is no direct nudging about this, but we pick it up, I think, unmistakably.

Stalker now proceeds to his rendezvous with Writer and Scientist, and together the men set out for the crossing. In the novel by the Strugatskys the border aspect isn't stressed, the Zone not being contiguous with a foreign country. In the film, however, the imagery of state boundaries is clear-cut. Stalker and his companions, as they slide their jeep out on to the railway tracks and follow the shunting engine through the automatic barrier, are fired upon by border guards. It is the sort of 'escape' sequence one has encountered in many war films, or in the Bond and Le Carré spy dramas. Is it far-fetched to imagine here that Tarkovsky is dreaming among other things his own departure to the West? At any event, the seriousness of Stalker's parting from his wife – her

*Like – but unlike – Susan Fleetwood's hysterical outburst in *The Sacrifice*.

In the Room: Scientist, Stalker, Writer

frenzied love and grief and his guilty moroseness – might seem to belong to this quasi-private world.

We now come to the imagery of the Zone itself. This belongs, I think, neither wholly to the East nor to the West. There are references to the Great Patriotic War. Tanks lie abandoned, overgrown with foliage, as they were abandoned over vast areas of Europe in the aftermath of 1945. Broken field telephones link up to forgotten observation posts, a technology of decay and desuetude. Equally, however, we appear to be in the aftermath of a nuclear explosion. Invisible pockets of radio-active land have to be circumnavigated by the Stalker's skilfulness. He whirls a series of bolt-weighted bandages ahead of him, like an Aborigine, to find his direction. All this, too, is 'inexplicit'. There is a curious absence of horror in the fields, the landscape being in fact strangely beautiful.

(Colour photography by Alexander Knyazhinsky emphasises the delicate blues and greens of the foliage.)*

In the last resort, however, there is simply a neutral allegorical background, a stage over which three different men pass in order to discover their destinies. An obvious comparison suggests itself with an opera like Mozart's *Magic Flute*. There aren't any demons or serpents, no Queen of the Night (no musical talisman) but the opera's corridors of fire and caves of ice find their filmic equivalent in the stalagmitic subterranean watercourses which have to be forded by the film's austere enquirers after truth. And in the shifting seas of earth and sand which hinder their passage, requiring to be fearlessly circumvented.†

Back, then, to allegory and art. And maybe this is where we should leave the matter. Beyond morality, beyond narrative, Tarkovsky's eye is, as we have said many times, the eye of the painter. Few film-makers have looked more patiently at the simple beauty of grass, moss, ferns and water. The last of these elements has often been mentioned, but perhaps there is more to be said about it. There is so much water in this film. In Tarkovsky's art reality would seem to have to be saturated in order to emerge into the world of appearance (like Japanese flowers that unfurl and bloom when one places them in a basin of water). There is perhaps an analogy here not only with painting, but with the process of photography itself: the sense in which the photographer in his darkroom lifts the treated paper from the chemical solution,

*I should relate what a friend from Moscow reported. When the film was shown in front of a native audience, no aspect of it was perceived as more allegorical than Stalker's whirling of the bolts in different oblique directions. The making of a detour of several miles to progress a mere hundred paces. 'Of course,' said my friend, 'that's *exactly* what life is like in the Soviet Union!'

†Mention of *The Magic Flute* (not capricious, I hope) brings to mind Ingmar Bergman, who both filmed the opera and, in *Hour of the Wolf*, provided a grim modern parable based upon it. I discuss Bergman more fully in relation to *The Sacrifice*, but one or two things can be said immediately. *Hour of the Wolf*, in its dark mood, denies that the humanism of Mozart's opera is any longer 'available' to us. 'When will my eye see the light?', as Tamino plaintively enquires; while the film seems to answer implacably 'Never!' What modern music there is on *Hour of the Wolf*'s soundtrack confirms, by its refusal of harmony, such an overall pessimism. In *Stalker* too there is a mixture of classical (mainly sacred) and modern music; but the two modes don't quarrel with each other. Tarkovsky here, as everywhere else, is marginally less anguish-ridden than the Swedish director. Music, as Stalker says, 'invades the soul', purifies it and opens it to beauty. The film ends, in fact, unironically, with a cracked, grainy excerpt from Beethoven's Ninth Symphony.

Scientist and the bomb

coaxing the image gently out into daylight. The wonderful water-dream sequence traces the course of a shallow stream with a variety of objects in it – cartons, pebbles, syringes, holy icons, coins. Water here evokes a treasured past, taking us back to the 'stuff' of the world, cleaning, protecting and polishing it into significance.*

*It seems too obvious to emphasise, but water is fabulously filmic. It can't surely be a coincidence that some of the greatest directors (Ozu, Mizoguchi, Renoir, Satyajit Ray) come back again and again to the image of water – either still or moving – to express their profoundest feelings about creativity and destructiveness.

Tentative conclusion
Stalker is frankly a difficult film. It brings up a number of problems of assessment. Sensing its awkwardness, Peter Green goes so far as to say, in an article in *Sight and Sound*, that it 'skirts hazardously close to hocus-pocus' (though he admires it).* Are we forced to agree, or to half-agree? Is there not a certain problem of portentousness? As Stalker threads his way through the radio-active minefield, the dangers lack an external embodiment which might allow us to appreciate his audacity. The film hovers always on the edge of parable, which some people find inimical to art.

On the other hand, there is for me little doubt about the film's greatness, related to its refinement and strangeness. Walls and houses and ruins are captured in the film with a Cézannian intensity. Tarkovsky becomes here (he is his own art director, in the strange Estonian landscape) one of the great contemporary artists of *poverty*, understood in its true spiritual sense:

> It is poverty's speech that seeks us out the most.
> It is older than the oldest speech of Rome.
> (Wallace Stevens, *To an Old Philosopher in Rome*)

Again (also from Wallace Stevens):

> Bare earth is best. Bare night is best. Bare, bare ...
> (*Evening Without Angels*)

There is this sense (since we are talking of painting), held by Cézanne of all modern artists, that great art belongs not to the drawing-room but 'down there, in the depths of the abyss'. *Stalker*'s melancholy is palpable, but clearsighted and unsentimental. For as Stalker's wife remarks in the profound final monologue: 'If there were no sorrow in life, it wouldn't be better; it would be worse!'

Influences: 1. Jean Cocteau
The imagery and momentum of *Stalker* – particularly the notion of transgression or journeying across to the 'Zone' – owe something, perhaps, to Cocteau's film *Orphée* (1950), which Tarkovsky had studied at film school. If the two films meet it is photographically in their style of hard-edged, black and white realism. The

---

*'The Nostalgia of the Stalker', *Sight and Sound*, Winter 1984–5.

architecture of the Zone in either case has a sort of neo-realist texture and shabbiness (scuffed walls, doors, muddy puddles, half-broken tiles).

Otherwise, I find that the films are not very similar. In Tarkovsky's work, no matter how allegorical the fable, real human relationships are countenanced – for instance that between husband and wife (who genuinely seem to love and to miss each other). Cocteau's film on the other hand is marked, I think, by its maker's inability to be honest about his fable's homosexual undertow. Why does Jean Marais make his fateful journey into the dangerous mirror-zone? Plainly, it is to *abandon* (not to fetch back) his wife Eurydice (Maria Déa), whom he despises with a special misogyny. Can we believe he loves the Death Princess Maria Casarès more than his handsome male companion Edouard Dermithe? The film comes unstuck on its emotional truth. It lacks (unlike Tarkovsky's) an underlying moral coherence. Cocteau couldn't find it in himself to be simple or pious enough; he couldn't (for all his intelligence) grasp the essence of the fable. This insincerity is not a fault attributable to *Stalker*, whatever the film's other faults may be.

2. Luis Buñuel

'To be simple enough or pious enough.' The simplicity of Luis Buñuel's film-making is well-known. Tarkovsky revered the Spanish director although it might seem at first sight that they were spiritually poles apart. The Spaniard's notorious atheism, as evidenced through the long years of his career from *L'Age d'or* (1930) to *Tristana* (1970), seemingly sets him at odds with the sincere, questing author of *Andrei Roublev*. Not only are they different 'spiritually', they are different in scale and ambition. Buñuel never contemplated an 'epic'. He tended to be funny or deprecating about the cinema's potential powers. The most it could offer, he said, was a 'keyhole' on to the world, a 'margin of alertness'. For years he claimed that film-making bored him.

And yet if we were to look for the filmic (as opposed to literary) origin of *Stalker* we might do worse than settle, in the end, for *Nazarin*. This is Buñuel's great film from the 1950s, concerning a priest's coming to grief as he attempts to lead the Christian life literally. At the simplest level, there are in *Stalker* recognisable quotations from this movie. The imagery of Alissa Freindlikh's fit – never properly explained in *Stalker* (for defensible artistic reasons) – makes reference, I think, to the epilepsy of the abandoned mistress in Buñuel's film. (The extraordinary force and

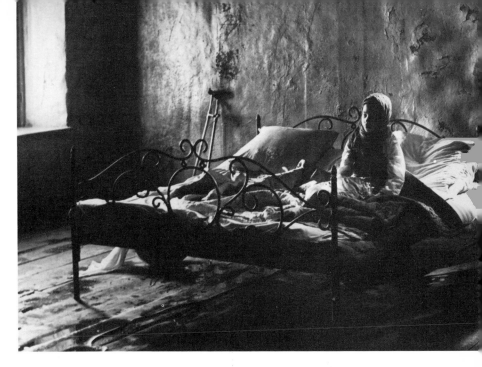

'A Cézannian intensity': Stalker's crippled daughter

purity of the woman's sexual longing is what is residually moving to Tarkovsky.)

The photographic aesthetic bareness of *Nazarin* is also well known: the dirty peeling walls of the priest's habitation where he nurses the wounded prostitute are like the bare plastered walls of Stalker's family billet. There is a zero-level poverty; but along with it a sort of acquired honesty in looking at the world, a grandeur that emerges from simplicity existing at the edge of nothingness. Buñuel's cinema is famous for its irony; but the irony in *Nazarin* is, for once, exceedingly restrained and 'sophisticated'. It is not even, in this case, anti-Christian. The dignity given to the priest protagonist, like the dignity given to Stalker, seems to me serious and compassionate.

In fact, in the end the real comparison between the two films resides (where it must reside) in the ethical sphere. Each film dramatises – with a discretion and lack of rhetoric which belong firmly with the finest art – a journey towards faith, at whose bitter end triumph and disillusionment become in their complexity indistinguishable.

NOSTALGHIA

Nostalghia (I spell the name in the way the film-maker asked us to) shared a Special Jury Award with Bresson's *L'Argent* at the 1983 Cannes festival, and the films were released in Britain shortly afterwards at much the same time. If the acclaim for Bresson was unanimous (more than one critic calling *L'Argent* 'the masterpiece of the 1980s'), one detected a certain critical disappointment with the Tarkovsky work. Both films are pessimistic, so it can't have been the gloominess of *Nostalghia* by itself which caused the critics' hesitation. Tarkovsky's film is longer than Bresson's, and narratively rather more complicated. But this doesn't of course make it better art. Was it that Tarkovsky's pessimism is formulated in a manner that is at least friendly towards religion, whereas Bresson's pessimism is atheist and absolute? Both films, whatever their differences of tone, seem to be about the relation of sanctity to madness. But it struck me when watching them that Tarkovsky, in his difficult way, was saying truer and better things about those concepts. Idea for idea, I think Tarkovsky's is the more serious work of art. But we should explore the ideas themselves before coming back to the question of verdicts.*

Narrative

Gorchakov (Oleg Yankovsky) is a Soviet musicologist who has been staying in Italy researching the life of an eighteenth-century Russian composer named Sosnovsky.† The research appears to be either over or coming to an end. Whether it has been successful or

---

*Reasons for not liking a work of art are seldom satisfying (though it is occasionally necessary to give them). For what it is worth, I state my reasons for mistrusting *L'Argent*'s apparent nihilism in 'Bresson, Tarkovsky and Contemporary Pessimism', *Cambridge Quarterly*, Summer 1984.

†Based on a genuine historical figure, Maximilian Beryózovsky (1745–77), author of the opera *Demofont*. 'He showed such musical ability that he was sent by his landowner to study in Italy, where he stayed many years, gave concerts and was much acclaimed. But in the end, driven no doubt by . . . inescapable Russian nostalgia, he eventually decided to return to serf-owning Russia, where, shortly afterwards, he hanged himself.' *Sculpting in Time* (p.203)

not in the conventional sense we are not told. The protagonist ought to be thinking of returning home – indeed he has powerful dreams of his wife and children – yet he lingers. As the film opens, he directs his beautiful Italian interpreter Evgenia (Domiziana Giordano) to visit a chapel he admires in the Tuscan hills. But their views on the meaning of this experience turn out to be quietly at cross purposes.

In the nearby spa village of Bagno Vignoni where they put up, still mildly quarrelling, Gorchakov becomes obsessed with the behaviour of a reclusive figure, Domenico (Erland Josephson), judged by the rest of the community to be mad. He visits him in his house outside the village and has long conversations. Later Domenico commits suicide by burning himself on top of the statue of Marcus Aurelius in Rome's Campidoglio, after a speech to assorted onlookers – some of whom look like fugitives from a mental hospital – on the dangers of nuclear catastrophe. Gorchakov, who is in Rome just before the immolation, cancels his air ticket and travels back to Bagno Vignoni by himself. There, in the drained thermal baths, he lights a candle that Domenico had given him and sets out to walk the thirty metres of the baths' length. It is as if the future of the world depended on his arriving at the far end without the candle guttering. Twice he sets out; twice the wind pinches the flame. But the third time – all this is shot in a long single uninterrupted take – he reaches the far end, where he collapses and, presumably, dies.

Such are the bare bones of the story. It is a history of crisis. The protagonist has three different relationships: first, with Italy (basically, a pull between Italy and Russia); secondly with Evgenia (a pull between her and his wife), and thirdly with Domenico. All three crises are interwoven, in the sense that the attraction towards Italy is also the attraction towards Evgenia (who in a certain sense symbolises her country); while conversely, in order to make up his mind about Evgenia, the hero will draw on ideas of faith that derive from his meetings with the recluse.

Exile, homesickness and Italy
Nostalgia means literally the pain for return: it is the traveller's ailment – the condition of exile. Yet in its peculiarly Russian form it is complicated by being part and parcel of its opposite, a sort of necessity for journeying that issues from Russia's enclosedness.

The ambivalent regard which educated Russians hold for the West is woven into its history on all levels, militarily, politically and culturally. We have already come across it briefly in this book in the allusion, when discussing *The Mirror*, to the debate between Pushkin and Chaadayev; Pushkin, than whom no one, in his personal culture, could be more deeply and grandly cosmopolitan, taking the Russian, patriotic view – that home is the best place of all – against Chaadayev's excessive Europhilism. Later in the 19th century the issue crops up again in Dostoevsky's distrust of Turgenev's rootlessness. (Dostoevsky himself, however, had lingered in the West, in those very spa towns he disparaged Turgenev for patronising.) At much the same time the Russian political émigrés, from Herzen to Lenin, came to possess invariably ambiguous attitudes – part curious, part hostile – about the West's sophistication and desirableness. After the Revolution, such ambivalence became if anything fiercer still. An invisible barrier now extended along the line of the frontiers. Those who had left were seen as 'enemies'. Those who remained found their only resort in dreaming of travel.

And dream they did. Osip Mandelstam invented for his poetry an imaginary Europe of the South, a classical continent that he named Colchis, stretching from the Black Sea round northern Turkey and into the Mediterranean. But as for travelling to those poetic regions, he disdained to beg Stalin's permission. The nearest he got was Armenia. Others conquered their pride, and for their pains were either refused, like Bulgakov (he requested to emigrate to Paris); or were suffered to travel abroad, like Bunin and Zamyatin, at the end of their lives, when they were known to be harmless or ill.

The catalogue of disappointments is long and well known. While selected publicists, musicians and performers have been permitted to make supervised visits, such exeats are at the government's pleasure, and always under the threat of revocation. Just to take one or two more celebrated names: Eisenstein, most international-minded of film-makers, was hauled back ignominiously from America; while Pasternak, Nobel laureate, was refused leave to travel to Stockholm. Mayakovsky, it is said, killed himself on hearing of Stalin's refusal to let him depart for France. A separate tragic category should be reserved for those, like the poet Marina Tsvetayeva and the novelist Isaac Babel, who returned from the safety of exile either to suicide or execution.

More recently, it must be said, and especially very recently, it seems as if matters have been getting freer. (They could scarcely have got less so.) Tarkovsky had first visited Italy in 1962 at the

A Russian abroad: Oleg Yankovsky as Gorchakov

time of the success of *Ivan's Childhood* at the Venice festival, where he met the writer Tonino Guerra, who extended an open invitation to return. Thus we find Tarkovsky in Italy again at the end of 1980, a free man – free, as he thought, to come and go from his country. He journeyed with Guerra round the south and north of the country, and made a short documentary about his experiences, *Tempo di viaggio* (unreleased in Britain and America). This documentary contained the germ of *Nostalghia*. The authorities at home, feeling liberal if apprehensive, agreed to become partners in a bigger project. *Nostalghia*, then, is an Italian-Russian co-production, begun in March 1981, made with money from Sovin Film on the Russian side and from RAI, the Italian state television company. To sympathetic outsiders, there was reason to be excited. Here for the first time for as long as anyone could remember was a Russian artist, who was not a dissident and not an émigré, moving magisterially into Europe with no strings attached, free to say exactly what he liked about it.*

The finished portrait of Italy is perhaps the film's first major problem. Critics have their own ideas about how a country should be photographed. If Italy is not merely a picture postcard background, it ought (so the argument runs) to transform the soul into happiness, as it had transformed the souls of all the great previous visitors from the North: Goethe, Stendhal, Keats, and so on. 'Kennst Du das Land wo die Zitronen blüh'n?' ('Do you know the country where the lemon trees blossom?'), asks Goethe. Alas, there aren't any lemon trees in *Nostalghia*, nor waving palms nor cerulean skies. The film's gloominess comes from a kind of resistance to Italy. The question that *Nostalghia* asks most simply is: can an artist survive and flourish in a country other than his own? Thus, while Italy contains its holy places – spots like the baths at Bagno Vignoni blessed by St Catherine of Siena, along with numerous beautiful churches, free and open for worship (unlike Russia's) – still, the real place of the heart, the place from which alone the artist draws sustenance and remains alive, is bound to be his own native land. This is the film's ideological 'statement', prosecuted with dignity and seriousness.

When the traditionalist Soviet director Sergei Bondarchuk (on the 1983 Cannes jury) did everything he could, with the backing of the Soviet authorities, to prevent *Nostalghia* winning the Palme d'or, Tarkovsky was able to point out that the film in fact stood for many things the authorities approved of. It was, he said, a patriotic film, made for Russians, about the impossibility of living in the West. That Bondarchuk's behaviour in the event actually forced Tarkovsky into the very exile he dreaded is too complicated a matter simply to be labelled an irony. The question at any event is not so much *can* an artist survive in another country (the success of

*We ought in fairness to make it clear that this was not the first time that such a thing had happened. Other Russian film directors have made films abroad before, but in 'safe' countries like Yugoslavia and Mexico, where nationality was not anyhow crucial to the story. Such films tend to be in the form of large-scale epics whose content and operating level offer no obvious ideological snares.

notable émigrés such as Nabokov proves it), as *should* he? Aren't his roots in a certain regard everything; aren't they priceless? Can the desire for one's country ever be deep enough, or passionate enough?*

Prayer, love and desire

The ambivalent attitude towards Italy which Gorchakov feels is centred on the figure of the interpreter Evgenia. If the relationship between her and the protagonist is at first to a certain extent allegorical, it becomes more thoughtful and realistic as the film progresses. (Can allegory by itself exist in an art-form like cinema,

*For the sequence of events surrounding *Nostalghia*'s reception at Cannes, see Angus McKinnon's interesting interview with the director, *Time Out*, 18 August 1984. Tarkovsky had expressed surprise that Bondarchuk, whose hostility was well known and attested, had been chosen by the authorities to represent the USSR on the Cannes jury. Reassurances from friends that the Soviet director had changed his tune and 'resolved to offer Tarkovsky support' did not in the event amount to much. In France, Bondarchuk remained his old self – 'fought like a tiger' against the giving of any awards to *Nostalghia*. Was it just Bondarchuk, or the higher authorities behind him? Tarkovsky came to realise, he said later, that the vote of Bondarchuk 'stood for' the vote of Goskino and the film authorities. Thus, subsequently to the fiasco, Tarkovsky wrote to Filip Yermash (Minister of Cinematography) and the head of the cultural section of the Central Committee asking politely for explanations of their obstructiveness. I have not seen these letters and cannot speak of their tone. I do know that they were not answered; nor later letters to Andropov and Chernenko. One has to consider in all this the blow to Tarkovsky's pride. He was a distinguished man with a fine career in cinema behind him. He had not, in his terms, done anything insulting to the state. On the contrary, his films were crafted, personal and as far as reasonable separate from politics. Now the highest powers were refusing to guarantee that he would ever find work again in his native land. What was he supposed to do? He had to live. With the 'greatest reluctance' Tarkovsky chose to stay on in the West. This reluctance was, of course, made fiercer still by the fact that his thirteen-year-old son Andrei had been refused leave to visit or join him.

The subsequent steps of Tarkovsky's career may conveniently be sketched at this point. West Berlin, Paris and London all offered themselves as places of possible domicile. Tarkovsky visited them; but having arrived in Italy he preferred to stay there, eventually buying a house for his family in Grosseto near Florence. By the summer of 1984 he had been planning *The Sacrifice* under the production aegis of the Swedish Film Institute and London's Channel Four. The decisive press conference announcing his 'defection' was in July 1984. The following months were difficult and unsettling. *Sacrifice* was shot between April and June 1985, editing completed by the beginning of 1986. By this time Tarkovsky was receiving treatment for cancer in Paris. Interceding on his behalf, President Mitterand – backed up by a press campaign in most of the European capitals – at last succeeded in persuading the Soviet authorities to let Tarkovsky's son and mother-in-law join him (January 1986). Tarkovsky died in Paris a year later, on 29 December 1986.

so plainly committed to the 'real'?) Evgenia is certainly beautiful. And Gorchakov, despite his moods, is in conventional terms a distinguished handsome visitor. Nothing, however, in the way of a consummated sexual affair occurs between the two. Why is this? Partly it is because, in terms of the film's scenario, Gorchakov is already married and in love with his wife; partly because, even if he were not, there seems to be something fundamental that is fated and impossible about the relationship. *Nostalghia* belongs to the quite large number of distinguished modern films – *L'Eclisse* (Antonioni, 1962), *Elisa, vida mía* (Saura, 1977), *Hour of the Wolf* (Bergman, 1968) are other works that spring to mind – which take as their task the exploration of an almost pathological breakdown between the sexes.

The films just mentioned are in their main thrust descriptive rather than diagnostic: they don't, that is, pretend to tell us *why* it is that love between men and women has become impossible (if indeed it has). Tarkovsky's film also does not claim to offer solutions; but it is slightly more forthcoming about the surmisable causes of the catastrophe. His diagnosis takes the form, I think, of a quite complicated critique of Western feminism (another reason, incidentally, for the film to be unpopular; for if feminism is going to be criticised, it had better be done, conventional wisdom has it, by feminists).

What is the critique, and does it really belong to Gorchakov or to Tarkovsky? Let us leave the second of these questions aside at the moment, and instead take up one or two pertinent observations about Evgenia's appearance. She is tall and broad-shouldered, ever so slightly aggressive in her walk. Her clothes announce a status of wealth and independence. They are couturier-designed and, in the fashion of the time, padded out with a redundancy of materials. Yet there is surely a flaw somewhere in her appearance. It is not anything so simple that she fails to carry off her chic, since she is as poised and confident as a model. But she is also somehow faintly ridiculous. In the hotel, she trips over her voluminous garments. In the Chapel of St Catherine (where the film opens) her high heels, combined with the carapace of costume, make it impossible for her to kneel down and pray. The film seems to be asking, through such negotiations, whether she can *submit herself* – implying that until men and women learn to 'humble' themselves, first in relation to God and then in relation to each other, there can be no proper cure for our disease.

The attitude towards prayer and kneeling which the film adopts is distinctive enough. Eliot famously commands his readers in *Four Quartets*: 'You are here to kneel/Where prayer has been valid.' (A country chapel, Little Gidding, like St Catherine's chapel in *Nostalghia*.) Yet in so far as the tone of Eliot's ordinance is peremptory, or priggish, we reply that thank you, we will make up our own minds. But *can* modern man kneel? is surely an interesting question. If the heroes of modern thought like Nietzsche, Freud or Marx seem at times to have disposed of the matter for ever, still there are other places in literature and art where the issue is more sympathetically encountered. In Rilke, in Tolstoy, in the private reflections of Wittgenstein, in some of the poems of Akhmatova and Tsvetayeva, we find an attitude towards inner meditation similar to the one shown in this film of Tarkovsky.*

Let us take these reflections a bit further. In the film's imagined Tuscan chapel where the action commences there is a famous painting by Piero della Francesca, the Madonna del Parto (Mad-

---

*Also in Thomas Mann: 'As far as I am concerned,' he says (*Reflections of a Non-Political Man*), 'I have always loved time spent in churches, specifically because of an aestheticism that had nothing at all to do with the study of culture and with handbook education, but that is rather directed toward what is human. Two steps aside from the amusing highway of progress, and you are surrounded by an asylum where seriousness, quiet and the thought of death have their proper places, and where the cross is raised for adoration. What a blessing! What *satisfaction*! Here one speaks neither of politics nor of business. The human being is a human being here, he has a heart and makes no secret of it. Here pure, liberated, nonbourgeois-solemn humanity rules. Here, before one's fellow men, one would be ashamed of rude words, of impudent conduct; but so strong is the right of the human being here, so complete the impotence of civil custom, that no one is ashamed before his fellow men of the expression and display of deep emotion, devotion, surrender and repentance, not even of a bodily posture that would provoke, in all civic situations, displeasure and laughter as theatrical, fantastic, eccentric and romantic. *The kneeling human being!* No, my humanity feels no displeasure in this picture. On the contrary, it suits it as does no other, specifically because of its anticivil, anachronistic, and daringly-human stamp. The posture appears nowhere else any more, it contradicts, in its relaxed humanity, all the reserve, scepticism, and hostility to gesture in "civilisation". Does the lover still kneel before his beloved when he woos her? How nakedly and terribly life in our times would have to break through the uniformity of "civilised" manners for one to see the human being who, on his knees, would hide his face in his hands, or raise his folded hands in front of him!' (Trans. Walter D. Morris, New York, 1983.) Once again, I feel the great prison memoirs of our century provide the sort of intense illumination that matters. In the spiritual biography of the wonderful Dutch writer Etty Hillesum – murdered by the Nazis at Auschwitz in 1943 – I notice that one of her projected, but unwritten, short stories is entitled 'The Girl Who Couldn't Kneel'.

Evgenia (Domiziana Giordano)

onna of Parturition). As Evgenia makes her way round the church a sacred ceremony is unfolding. Scarved peasant girls and women congregate by a maze of candles. At a given moment, one of the supplicants lets a flock of starlings out of the belly of a statue of the Madonna. Boldly the sacristan asks Evgenia whether she has come to pray to have a child, or to be spared a child. The shallow evasiveness of Evgenia's answer ('I'm just looking', as in a department store) reinforces the troublesomeness of the question. 'What *are* you here for, then?' The reply of the sacristan may on this occasion be taken to be Tarkovsky's: '*A woman is meant to have children, and to raise them with patience and self-sacrifice.*'

All this is fantastically ideological; and we can only repeat the qualification that Gorchakov, though plainly standing for things the director approves of, is not in fact the director himself. The feelings and beliefs of the protagonist are situated in a play of *other* feelings and beliefs, among which Evgenia's own have a balancing force and importance.

This becomes clear enough in the powerful and important scene showing her tirade in the hotel bedroom. Gorchakov has returned from a visit to Domenico. Evgenia is sitting on his bed, drying her hair. (Her excuse for being there is that the water has run out in her own bathroom.) When Gorchakov shows her the candle Domenico has given him, her long-tested patience seems to snap. She'd like to sleep for ten days and wipe him out, she cries. She calls him a vile stupid coward, exclusively interested in saints and madonnas. In Moscow there were many fine Russians: why did she have to end up interpreting for this one? Isn't he a sort of soft worm, with legs, that gets stuck in one's hair in a nightmare? The speech, delivered weeping and with bared breast, is a marvellously human cry of passion, an *erotic* cry from the body against Gorchakov's withdrawn cerebration. In its frankness, directness and integrity it gives a reminder, if the point needed making, that, dramatically speaking, this is a contest between equals.

In fact, of course, a current of strong sexual feeling does subsist between Gorchakov and Evgenia irrespective of their quarrels and silences. Dream sequences underline this. One moment Gorchakov dreams of her as an annunciatory angel chastely kissing his wife on the cheek; yet the next moment in his fantasy she is lying on top of him in erotic abandon. *Nostalghia* isn't specifically 'about' human sexuality in the way that the films of Bergman, Antonioni and Saura are. But Tarkovsky, I think, knows the human body sufficiently. Despite its repressions (perhaps because of them) the film has a physical existence, a 'knowledge' of men and women that counterbalances its austere meditation.*

Madness and sanctity

The enigmatic figure in the film is of course Domenico. What are we to make of his actions and his speeches? We learn from the flashbacks that he has been obsessed for many years with visions of apocalypse. At first he thought it was right to do what he could privately to safeguard his family. With this in mind he imprisoned them in his house for a period of seven years. (The villagers, who have eventually caused the wife and children's rescue, thought the

---

*It may be objected by feminists that the fantasies are all on Gorchakov's side, not on Evgenia's. A hostile critique might further claim that the idealisation of women that is involved in them is pitched at a solemn or ridiculous level of purity: Gorchakov turns his women into angels. What, if there is one, is the equivalent idealisation that a woman makes of the man she loves? The provisional limit to such enquiries is met when we remind ourselves that Tarkovsky, after all, is a male director. A woman's view would be – a woman's view. One would hope nonetheless that there is a middle area which is emotionally comprehensible to both men and women.

'Alone, discredited, a recluse': Domenico (Erland Josephson)

motive was jealousy.) Now alone, discredited, a recluse, he believes it more than ever his duty to 'speak out' to the world. Gorchakov will lend a willing ear. Domenico is ambitious for a supreme act of witness. Thus, making his way to Rome, he sets fire to himself from the top of the equestrian statue of Marcus Aurelius.

These actions are, of course, at one level, straightforwardly the actions of a madman; but this is not how the film invites us to perceive them. On the contrary, it seems to be asking at times whether madness is not another name for sanctity. Domenico dies sincerely for his faith in the possibility of mankind's repentance. In antique and medieval times many martyrs went to similar deaths joyfully. We live now in a humanitarian age, where such gestures are thought to be exhibitionist (though this does not mean they don't happen: more people than the present writer perhaps can remember being moved by the death of Jan Palach in Czechoslovakia). What is odd at first sight about *Nostalghia* is Tarkovsky's reluctance to pathologise Domenico's intense self-defeating piety. Might it not be, he asks, that the force of such gestures gives obscure meaning to the world; sheds, even, indispensable light on our condition? Plainly not everyone will wish to go along with this; but, as with the film's thoughts about exile and marriage, one can submit that the proposition is serious.

At any event, the flame is distributed through the film at many different levels, most obviously in the exchange between the human torch of Domenico's sacrifice and the sacerdotal candle – paradoxical image of hope – which Gorchakov carries across the baths cupped in his hands (like an image out of Dürer). The candle in turn takes us back in recollection to the massed bank of tapers surrounding the statue of the Virgin in the Chapel of St Catherine (as the saint reminds us of her namesake on the wheel).* There are other fierce flames in the film, for example the matutinal sun that burns over the Russian hills. And there is the vision of Gorchakov standing drunk in a mossy stream, a candle consuming the page of the poem that is being recited in voice-over:

> I'm a candle burnt out at a feast.
> Gather my wax up at dawn,
> And this page will tell you the secret
> Of how to weep and where to be proud,
> How to distribute the final third
> Of delight, and make an easy death.
> Then, sheltered by some chance roof,
> To blaze, word-like, with posthumous light.
>
> (Translation: Kitty Hunter Blair)

'To blaze, word-like, with posthumous light': if Domenico (rather than Gorchakov) has a serious wish beneath his madness it is this. Overall the images of flame – the belief in flame's efficacy – qualify the film's deadly melancholy, restoring something of sanity and ambiguity to the madman. If the film is clearly in some sort a death wish (Domenico's, Gorchakov's, Tarkovsky's even), the death desire here consorts, I believe, with a serious and dignified hope for humanity.†

---

*There are two Saint Catherines in the Christian calendar. St Catherine of Alexandria was the (firework) martyr. However, the fourteenth century St Catherine of Siena – friend of popes and emperors, tireless campaigner for world peace – is the underlying sacred presence in the film.

†This in fact is my exclusive reason for preferring *Nostalghia* to *L'Argent*. In *L'Argent* the pessimism is absolute. Yet the film pretends it isn't so by adopting a cadence of religion. Bresson makes a rapture out of nihilism and this seems to me in bad taste.

Then does the character of Domenico 'come off' psychologically? I think there are one or two problems. The main one is that there is an insufficient sense of his extraordinariness. Josephson, the actor, has powerful and haunted features; and the words used to express his apprehension possess, again, an adequate poetry. (This is particularly true of the suicide speech from the statue, with its dense imagery and cryptic exhortation.) Yet despite this, it is arguable that simply not enough is shown of the man. The audience never quite arrives at the stage where it can pity or empathise with him properly.

Must madness then always be opaque? In Bergman's remarkable chamberpiece *Persona* (1966), the question is left open throughout as to whether Liv Ullmann's nervous breakdown is genuine or motivated by malice. (She cruelly refuses, if we remember, to speak to her nurse and companion Bibi Andersson.) As the film progresses, however, the question is resolved by the greater and greater depths of the actress' humanity. In the end, and having journeyed through the blackest despair, there can be little doubt that we are in the presence of a genuine human compassion – witnessing, suffering, growing in steadfastness.

Likewise, a comparison could be made with Rossellini's fine film *Europa 51* (alternative title: *The Greatest Love*), in which a rich and hitherto spoiled young mother (Ingrid Bergman) suffers a mental breakdown after the accidental death of her son. At this point she casts off her attachment to the world, throwing in her lot with the poverty-stricken. The film follows what would conventionally be called her 'decline' to the point where she is incarcerated in a mental hospital (only to insist on remaining there voluntarily when the opportunity comes for her release). Her language becomes more and more 'difficult', like Domenico's. *Europa 51*, though, has perhaps this major advantage over *Nostalghia*'s scenario, that in delineating the character of a modern refulgent saint, it refers us to actions – of charity, compassion and self-effacement – which the audience can clearly recognise as holy. In *Nostalghia* the problem at bottom resides with Domenico's goodness. *Is* he good? Maybe he is. But the film has rather too many other strands to come out one way or another convincingly. Rossellini's and Bergman's films convince (apart from intrinsic reasons) because a single central theme is being followed.

All this may seem exterior (I hope it does not). Arguing in favour of the film we should say that as well as seriousness there is a humour which ought not be ignored. From his first enigmatic

'With posthumous light': Gorchakov with the candle

confrontation with Evgenia (blasphemously quoting Christ's words to St Catherine: 'You are she who is not. I am he who is') through his later silences and severities – including the strange, crucial hour spent with Gorchakov in the draughty barn (half romantic landscape, half human habitation) – to the moment of his death, we are kept alive to Domenico's elusive dangerousness. Is he a Holy Fool, a saint? Or one of those hyperactive conspirators from Dostoevsky? The film wants us not to know. It wants us to *puzzle out* the content of the man's spirituality.

Towards a conclusion
An exegetical critic can't help being aware of the betrayal involved in the fact that the cinema is a visual, sensuous medium. An idea, in the cinema, is a camera movement, not a speech. *Nostalghia* has its fair share of orations; but just as importantly, it has its fair share of

silence and contemplation. Here Tarkovsky's camera, restlessly moving over nature and stone and human physiognomy, forges an inexpressible discourse beyond ethics. The physical universe of *Nostalghia* is as detailed, concrete and imagined as any of Tarkovsky's great previous films. We come back to the really extraordinary density with which Tarkovsky manages to infuse objects. As they emerge on the screen, nature and landscape seem to take on a history, a meaning, a vibration. This is the reason why, despite the film's apparent melancholy, one can't really rest a case on its pessimism. It is too 'mastered' to be wholly unhappy. An artist, we are inclined to say, could not have filmed the world as Tarkovsky does here unless he was partly in love with it. The film-maker's mastery is observable in all his usual perfectionism, in those wonderful transitions between dream, flashback and reality. The calcium-encrusted objects in the Baths (bicycles, bottles) are like memories washed up from the tombs of archaeology, infused with the sense of hidden riches.

In the end there is Italy itself, captured not luxuriously, but appropriately. There are, as we have said, no Goethian lemon trees; but the landscape has its austere level of majesty. The scenes in Rome are filmically organised – Saint Peter's from the Palatine monumental and ancient, like the buildings and museums round the Campidoglio. Care has been taken to achieve 'texture'. Tarkovsky was a great sensuous artist; and the substrate of his vision (glimpsed in the extraordinary last shot of the cathedral-enclosed dacha) takes in the materials of nature: light, stone, water, wood and snow.

Antonioni, Guerra, Tarkovsky

The scenario for *Nostalghia* was written by Tarkovsky in conjunction with the leading Italian scriptwriter Tonino Guerra. (They had met in 1962, drawn together by the fact that Guerra has a Russian wife.) The Italian's distinguished career includes at least two films for Michelangelo Antonioni, *L'Eclisse* (*The Eclipse*, 1962) and *Identification of a Woman* (1982). These movies form an interesting contrast to *Nostalghia*, and might be commented on further.

Do I mean contrast or comparison? All three films look with great intensity at a surmised moral breakdown between the sexes. Each is about love's 'impossibility'. In *L'Eclisse* the conflict is between a sophisticated modern woman who works, like Evgenia, as a translator (Monica Vitti); and a dashing young broker on the

Milan stock exchange (Alain Delon). The film is brilliant for its depiction of a love affair that almost works out, but doesn't quite. The desolation of spirit known as *ennui* becomes dramatised with a paradoxical passion. No one is blamed for the impasse. The film is (contrary in certain ways to Tarkovsky's) unideological: seen not only from Delon's side, but from Vitti's.

Twenty years later (and a year before the making of *Nostalghia*) Guerra wrote *Identification of a Woman*. In this film the problem of relating between the sexes is sensed, more or less explicitly, to founder on a sort of pervasive androgyny. The protagonist is confronted in his sexual life with a choice: between a heterosexual young woman and a slightly older woman who, however, is significantly lesbian. It is the latter who intrigues him particularly. But the identity of a woman, the film implies, by coming closer, in her independence, to a man's, becomes correspondingly harder to 'complement'. The film queries the social conditions that contrive to bring about such a state of affairs. Its problem, though, is that it doesn't know this profoundly. *Identification of a Woman* lacks the indefinable moral gracefulness of *L'Eclisse*. For if in the earlier work marriage was still seen as an ideal (even as it could not be implemented) the later work, by contrast, carries an insufficient sense of the adult moral life of men and women, and collapses in an impotent hedonism.

Nostalghia, then, takes over from *Identification of a Woman* its diagnosis of our sophisticated modern plight. But the Russian film differs from the Italian in possessing a rather more severe moral passion – in fact a puritanism – a certain grim hostility towards 'pleasure'. Gorchakov says to Evgenia at the Chapel: 'I'm sick of these "beautiful sights". I want nothing more just for myself.' Wanting nothing more 'just for oneself' means, in Tarkovsky's terms, living morally, according to the tenets of Christian tradition. *Nostalghia* meditates, by default, on the value and virtue of monogamy. Whether we agree with Tarkovsky's private views is, of course, an individual matter: at any event, beyond the legitimate bounds of film criticism.

THE SACRIFICE

The achieved, magisterial quality that is felt about Tarkovsky's last film is not to be separated from its difficulty. The film is a realistic parable, which ought to point in the direction of simplicity. Yet the meaning of the parable remains teasingly out of reach, like one of those dreams which while being experienced has the greatest lucidity but on waking dissolves into vagueness. The question the viewer is left with is: to what extent is the sacrifice which the title speaks of *didactic*? One that we should follow? Outside the film, in his interviews in the months before his death Tarkovsky gave out contradictory signals, on the one hand declaring, as if nothing were simpler, that sacrifice is *the* overriding human quality which separates man from the beasts; on the other hand reserving his position. 'The artist as a man is passionate,' he said (rather like T. S. Eliot), 'but he resolves his passions into the forms that he creates. At any event, to "put one's own sentiments" into a work of art is vulgar.' ('A Propos "The Sacrifice"', 15 March 1986). What is the film actually saying about sacrifice? Is it a morality we agree with?

Let us remind ourselves: in ancient times a sacrifice was a propitiation. The ox or the garlanded ram was killed on the altar as thanksgiving for some benediction, or else to placate the gods in the pursuit of events which, otherwise, stood a chance of turning out badly. The movement from pagan superstition, with its own poetic morality, to the later moral system of Christianity involves above all the recognition that the sacrifice does not have to be 'literal'. It is an offering that you yourself make, of yourself, rather than of a third party or scapegoat. Yet the issue still carries with it problems of fairness and justice, in the sense that it can't help affecting other people, in a way that redounds on *their* freedom.

This, on the surface, is the immediate problem one finds set up in Tarkovsky's film. A brief résumé of the events. A nuclear war looks as if it is going to be unleashed. Jets fly low, and with deafening noise, over the deserted part of Sweden where a distinguished theatre man, Alexander (Erland Josephson), lives with his ex-actress wife Adelaide (Susan Fleetwood), infant son

Gossen ('Little Man', Tommy Kjellqvist) and teenage daughter
Marta (Filippa Franzén). Also there are a servant, Julia, and
neighbours Otto (a bicycling postman), Victor (perhaps Adelaide's
lover), and a mysterious Icelandic woman, Maria.

At a precise moment in the terror-stricken summer night,
Alexander makes a private vow to God that if he and his family can
only live through the hours until dawn, he will break off all human
connections and live henceforth in silence and solitude. There
follows a separate, semi-hysterical episode involving the Icelandic
woman (a sort of holy adultery, urged on by Otto). The outcome is
that they all do get through the night. So that by the time morning
comes the bargain is ready to be put into effect.

This bargain takes the shape of a series of manoeuvres that have
not been explicitly foreseen in the vow. Thus Alexander lures his
family off on a walk to the shoreline, then behind their backs sets
fire to the house and its contents. The horrified return of his loved
ones – along with Alexander's crazy bounding around as he
attempts to explain, and yet not explain – forms the substance of a
final virtuoso sequence, discussed presently.

It seems to me that Alexander's promise becomes complicated,
from our point of view, on account of its unilateral basis: it is *his*
renunciation, not his family's. Yet the flaming pyre initiates a
suffering which logically is just as much theirs as his. Can sacrifice
be sacrifice if it implicates innocent people? To put my question
another way: is this the sacrifice which, in speaking of a 'didactic'
work of art, we would specify as clear or sublime?

It would be tedious to make a full list of the film's ambiguities,
but some of the other key points of complication should nonetheless be alluded to. The first of these might be described as an
uncertainty about the background of the bargain. Psychologically,
two different things appear to be going on at the same time. On the
one hand, there is Alexander's fear of nuclear apocalypse. On the
other, there is what we might call a private, or existentialist, crisis
burning in him about his relationship with his wife, and her
relationship with their friend Victor (Sven Wollter). The marital
and the political/historical problems unite to cause one
momentous dark night of the soul. Judged, however, in sober
moral terms, these crises surely have an utterly different weight.
We can put it most simply by saying: it is one thing to sacrifice
yourself and your family to save the world from being consumed in
a fireball; it is another thing entirely to sacrifice them merely to
assuage private feelings of guilt and revenge.

'A benevolent witch, a holy innocent': Alexander and the foreign woman

This is one of the key things the film is vague about, we must assume deliberately. We can fill this out in various ways, by noticing, for example, that there is not one special bargain, but two. In the first, Alexander sinks to his knees and addresses to God the profound prayer for survival the terms of which have already been alluded to. But later in the night there is the second encounter. Otto (Allan Edwall), the crazy postman, buttonholes Alexander in an upstairs room and tells him of a privately held vision. Here the 'sole terms of survival' for them (and perhaps the rest of the world) are that Alexander shall visit the house of the mysterious foreign woman Maria (Gúdrun Gísladóttir) and sleep with her. She is, says Otto, 'waiting for him', like a saint from the Bible ('Lie with her! Convince her!'). Alexander obeys, and his obedience brings into being one of the mysterious key scenes of the film. Yet we may ask, I think, when it is over and the morning arrives, whether it is the Visit or the Prayer (or neither) that is the cause of their ultimate survival.

Perhaps, we are allowed to think, they would all have survived until morning anyway. The extravagance of a deep vow is an integral part of its economy and meaning. At any event, the possibility of destiny's indifference to Alexander's petition (the quarrelling nations had anyway made up their differences) is an option which the film holds open for us. While Alexander prays, there is a legitimate question as to whether he is praying *to* anything. Is God present or absent in this film? We are never really sure what the director thinks on this matter. All we can begin to surmise is that the drama exists on a somewhat different plane from that of a homily.

In fact, the more we look at it the more it seems possible that what *The Sacrifice* is after is to capture pure poetic states of soul. As clearly as in the plays of Chekhov or the films of Bergman, the imperative is to keep the characters ambiguous. Who are they? Impossible to pin them down in terms of gesture or status. The postman, Otto, appears to be conversant with Nietzsche and chiromancy. The little child is both mascot of innocence and wounded demonic goblin. The foreign woman Maria doubles, as we have seen, as servant and a sort of benevolent Mary Magdalene; while the maid Julia (Valérie Mairesse) is a tenderer mother to the child than the real mother Adelaide. If the film has a power and initial intrigue (and I think it has) it resides where it always resides in Tarkovsky, in the faces and bearing of the actors: in their vulnerability, mystery and beauty.

Still, we have to get back to the question of sacrifice, because the film hinges on it. We may agree, so far, on what it is not: sacrifice, in Tarkovsky's film, is not the simple Christian selflessness associated with modern heroes of the spirit (like Mother Teresa in Calcutta). Nor is it the profound stoic abnegation – the *self*-sacrifice – that we find in the novels of Henry James, or in the cinema of Ozu and Mizoguchi. In so far as it can be pinned down in words its meaning would seem to be formal: it is the moment of crisis in a man's or a woman's personal life, the moment of *clarification* which issues in irrevocable decision. When the film opens, Alexander is a man seemingly lost in irony and scepticism. His sophistication has not brought him happiness. The threatened arrival of total war takes on, for him, the form of an astonishing personal opportunity. Suddenly everything becomes lucid, as if his life had been one long preparation for this moment. Alexander's bargain with God, in short, is the discovery of a destiny. At last he thinks he understands what he is on earth for.

We wonder whether in real life this is a profound moment or a dangerous one. Destiny so often means lordliness, even tyranny. Fortified in a belief in his 'vision', a man can contemplate leaving behind traditional moral norms. A similar *équivoque* is the basis of Nicholas Ray's melodrama *Bigger Than Life* (1956), where the James Mason character, under the influence of the drug cortisone, comes to think of himself as the reincarnated prophet Abraham. His task being 'revealed' to him, everyone must follow his bidding. Terribly and implacably he prepares to mete out punishment to his erring son. (Wife, pleading: 'God changed his mind about the sacrifice.' Mason, holding a pair of scissors: 'God was mistaken!') Does the solipsist's paranoia also attach to Alexander's actions? What makes *The Sacrifice* so 'difficult' is that there is no clear way open to us of judging either his sanity or his sobriety. (We have noticed, I think, a similar problem with Domenico in *Nostalghia*.)

In a filmed interview with Donatella Baglivo, Tarkovsky came up with the observation that to know who you are (in that utterly complete way suggested by the discovery of a destiny) is the prerequisite both for living rightly and for loving other people: 'He who doesn't know *why* he is here on earth cannot feel love for anyone else.' We may profoundly agree with this sentiment, and still not feel that it is essentially exemplified in *The Sacrifice*. For Alexander's self-discovery is a dead end: it fails to issue in proper human solidarity. The despair of the film (compared even to a film like *Nostalghia*) may be measured by the fact that marriage in particular – the staple human relationship so beautifully and calmly portrayed in Tarkovsky's earlier films – is turned away from, with a private and mysterious disgust. (As played by Susan Fleetwood, Adelaide, the wife of Alexander, is surely the least sympathetic of all Tarkovsky's women characters.) Here the relationship with the foreign woman Maria (a benevolent witch, a holy innocent) can't really substitute for the intelligence and warmth of characterisation that we have found in Tarkovsky's previous films. It seems significant to me that Alexander's seduction of her is rather tortuous and unconvincing. A rambling monologue about mistakenly ruining his mother's garden and shearing his sister's hair never quite locks into relevance. The scene has a mechanical mysticism about it, as if the film-maker, almost for the very first time, were tiring of inspiration. Nor, I think, is this mitigated by the actress' grave, quiet tenderness.

'A sense of dream': the house in the wilderness

I repeat, however, my opening observation, that *The Sacrifice* is undoubtedly magisterial. Despite the above strictures there is a gloomy perverse authority about this final film of Tarkovsky's, whose dramatisation of the fear of death loosens, in retrospect, a number of unhappy ironies. Did its director when he made it know he was dying? It is possible. The film seems to me to engage as powerfully as ever with a specific, mastered metaphysics of cinema. There is no falling off in Tarkovsky's mysterious ability to create a concrete human environment, and to people it with intense, passionate characters.

Let us notice, first of all, the house itself, in its corner of the wilderness, a timber-frame construction two storeys high, sur-rounded by pine trees, with a balcony facing away from the ocean. (Essentially it is the same design as the dacha in *Solaris*.) The conversations that take place through the film's long night permit us to know its ground plan in detail. Like all Tarkovsky's houses, it is governed by a logic of mirrors. Upstairs there is a sitting-room monopolised by the two men, Alexander and Otto. Entry seems to be through the outside window of the balcony, in turn connected to the ground by a ladder placed against the wall of the house. Yet at other times the two men descend the spiral staircase connecting the upstairs landing to the downstairs parlour, in which the bulk of the drama unfolds. The effect of this circular and vertical nexus of entrances and exits is to help create a sense of dream, of unease – as in those perpetual motion drawings of Escher where, on a staircase, the characters are at the same time coming up and going down. The invariably mobile camerawork of the film is engaged in two contradictory manoeuvres, creating on the one hand a spatial integrity (we are on stage, with no cuts or editing, constrained to suffer both the boredom and epiphanies of real time), on the other hand causing a *dislocation*, in the constant confusing interplay of inside and outside, upstairs and downstairs, real image and mirror reflection.

In *The Sacrifice*, too (to continue these thoughts about form), Tarkovsky seems to take further than ever his experiments with the extended sequence shot. The wonderful opening shot – so simple and lucid – has the camera standing back to observe Alexander helping his son plant a Japanese tree on the shoreline. When Otto appears with his telegram (from the 'Ricardians', celebrating Alexander's fiftieth birthday), the camera tracks slowly leftward, following the two talking men, Otto still on his bicycle, the little child holding Alexander's hand. As Otto dismounts, the child clandestinely attaches a rope to his mudguard, causing the bicycle, on the postman's leave-taking, to topple over comically. (Why, after seeing the film five or six times, do I still find this shot so enticing, convincing, *real?*)

Second sequence (or half-sequence: 'interlude'): another essay in panning, this time from the middle of the film. There is a sound of two jet planes, separated by an interval of seconds, diving over the house. The camera moves left to right across the room, passing in front of a glass cabinet in which jars and plates are shaking, and in particular a large receptacle which looks as if it contains milk. As the camera moves back in a reverse pan following Marta's frightened exit, the shaking gets worse. A final reverse as Julia enters combines with a zoom into the cabinet at exactly the moment when the jug crashes to the ground, spattering its contents across the floorboards.

Third sequence: the extraordinary scene of the burning of the house. Alexander in his dressing-grown, having shaken off his family, piles wicker chairs on the table in the conservatory, covering the makeshift sculpture with a white linen tablecloth. Two attempts are made to light the torch, the second succeeding. Then we are outside, the camera standing far back, as in the middle distance the squatting Alexander (his back towards the camera) looks on in satisfaction at the slowly burning house. Cries from his running relatives, and the camera dollies right; so Alexander hares off in the opposite direction, the camera following, to the point where Maria has taken up isolated station with her bicycle. Then more dollying, as a hastily summoned ambulance arrives (all this, of course, in the same single shot) and Alexander, half-praying, half-explaining, allows himself to be bustled into it. As the ambulance moves off, its path describes a particular arabesque taking the burning house once more back into the centre of the image, just at the moment when its frame topples over with a crash towards the screen. On the camera travels, to pick up Maria again, mounting her bicycle and splashing off, direction right, in pursuit of the ambulance. (This entire shot lasts five and three-quarter minutes.)*

Each of these sequences involves a balance, a precariousness: a bicycle that topples, a jar that smashes, a house that disintegrates. Each has its own internal suspense and climax. Above all, each might, of course, have been more swiftly and efficiently filmed by being cut up, in the conventional manner, into a series of separate matched 'takes'. Yet in so far as this last is concerned, narrative smoothness – efficiency in the telling of the story – seems no longer to be the issue in *The Sacrifice*. Tarkovsky takes us back by his method of seamless single shot to the earliest wonders of deep-focus silent film-making: to a sort of contentless fascination with time and movement itself. The human body is seen engaged in the simplest tasks: walking, conversing, running, reacting. The shots summon up the poignancy of the earliest documentaries. From another perspective, they burlesque the silent comic masters.

Then again, we can't help noticing how 'theatrical', too, *The Sacrifice* is, much more so than any of Tarkovsky's other films. Nor is this merely because the protagonist is a retired theatre man with a liking for Shakespeare, and married to a former English stage actress. It is surely connected to the manner in which the dialogues themselves are imagined. The bare floorboards of the

---

*For a detailed and entertaining description of the making of this complex sequence (it had to be shot twice), see Lars-Olof Löthwall's article in *Positif* no. 303, May 1986.

The burning house

austere, carpetless house exaggerate the clacking of the mother's and daughter's high heels on the soundtrack and the rustle of their dresses (dresses which anyhow share something of the artificiality of stage costume). In his early career (at the time, say, of *Andrei Roublev*) Tarkovsky was an implacable enemy of 'theatre'. But perhaps in the end he had come to think better of his position. And who are we to say, concerning great films like Dreyer's *Ordet* or Renoir's *La Règle du Jeu*, whether their power belongs essentially to the theatre or to the cinema? At a certain level of profundity the traditions of the one move seamlessly into the traditions of the other.* So the 'staginess' of *The Sacrifice* combines, harmoniously enough I think, with the purest filmic naturalism. It has a

---

*André Bazin has cogent observations on this complicated point of aesthetics in a marvellous essay, 'Theatre and Cinema' (*What is Cinema?*, vol. 1.)

simplicity such as we have seldom seen, even in Tarkovsky's previous work. We might specify such scenes as the discussion of the meaning of the icons in the book which Victor has given Alexander as a birthday present. Here an off-screen hand turns the pages and smoothes the illustrations in close-up. It is almost like a college slide lecture. And similarly, when Otto bicycles over from the village with his present, a large seventeenth-century map of Europe, there is a crystal-clear ease of *mise en scène* as the characters gather round and comment on the gift. The simplest human actions find pellucid classical expression in *The Sacrifice*, almost as if the arranging of such tableaux (Adelaide's tearing up of a letter at the breakfast table, Maria outside turning away from Alexander in the twilight, Marta's naked form reflected in the bedroom mirror) is the essential matter that moved the director, and not the philosophical subtext.

In short, it seems to me simplicity and complexity lie back to back in this last great, tragically flawed film of Tarkovsky's. Throughout, there is an effort towards paring down; a research into directness of expression; a reliance on 'unities', classicism, the mute power of landscape. At the same time there is mystery and poetry. Mystery, of course, can mean many things: it can be an alibi for hollowness and confusion. But you don't (at least I don't) ultimately feel this constriction about *The Sacrifice*'s opaque 'indecipherability'.

One or two final observations on form and content. Music first, and importantly (for I have not discussed music much in relation to Tarkovsky's other films). There are the three different registers, all harmonising: sacred (Bach's Matthew Passion played over the opening credits and final images); modern Japanese flute (played by Alexander on his tape recorder); thirdly, the plaintive Swedish shepherd song sung in a woman's semi-yodelling soprano voice, piercing the film at certain moments as if heard from the distance, like the cry of a peewit or seagull. Such 'vibrations' (they are literally that) connect up, of course, to Tarkovsky's obsession with the truths that lie beyond language. Their combination is as unique, as uncommentable, as the northern summer light in which the film is bathed – and like that light, poised delicately between ecstasy and despair.

Painting. The film focuses on a print of a great unfinished painting by Leonardo situated in the upstairs sitting-room. We see it first behind the opening credits. The Virgin is surrounded by three gift-bearing kings. One of them holds up a casket (signalling

'Gossen' and the sacred tree

the film's special theme: sacrifice, offering, humility). Towering
over them, a beneficent tree shades the sacred figures. The tree in
turn moves forward into the narrative proper (whose opening
scene shows the planting of another sacred tree).

Yet nothing is so straightforward as it seems. The Magi, when
we look at them, have demonic, goblin-like countenances. The
painting, under another aspect, is malicious and sinister – seeming
to tie up with the little boy himself, Alexander's son, 'Gossen',

recovering from his throat operation: in some sense also a dwarf-goblin or freak. (There is the hoarse voice, and the curious wound on his neck.) It is not contradictory that Gossen is in fact what he seems: a charming young six-year-old, through whose recovery of speech the film offers its final message of humanism and hope. For the mysterious layer of unease has been added – layer of sorcery, occultism, cinema.

Dostoevsky

Invocation of the name of Dostoevsky in reference to these late films of Tarkovsky may seem in danger of becoming automatic. Yet mentioning him one last time allows me to make explicit what in previous references was left stranded in allusion. The film's puzzling morality is surely linked to the Dostoevskian tradition, and in particular to that insouciance about material possessions that one finds markedly in the hero of *Notes from Underground*, who sees the 'most advantageous of advantages' in doing exactly as he likes, even if it is against his own interests. Alexander's burning of the house and family possessions, which under a certain light seems (to the bourgeois critic) so blasphemous and imprudent, is part of an ancient Russian protest against overweening control: against a society which, in its modern incarnation, egregiously claims to satisfy all the needs of its citizens. There are material needs; but what of the spiritual ones? Sacrifice here is a *gesture*, important as such, not for the reason it is done for. The position, though odd, is a rational one.

And then again, don't we also want to say that the greatness of Dostoevsky is essentially a greatness of *comedy*? So it may be, finally, with the problem of didacticism which I opened this chapter by speculating on. Alexander and Otto are a typical pair of quarrelling Dostoevskian intellectuals. The terrible sincerity with which Alexander pursues his destiny resides, in turn, with the music-hall clumsiness of his gestures, with his futility, his pathos. Drink is a vital part of his psyche. It fuels his prophecy, supplies wit and sardonic edge to his aphorisms. Both Otto and Alexander are great-spirited, but at the same time credulous and mad. The nobility of Alexander's sacrifice finally moves us, even in relation to what we may harbour against its wisdom.

Tarkovsky and Bergman

Ingmar Bergman's great admiration for Tarkovsky is a matter of record. Likewise, of course, *The Sacrifice* is Tarkovsky's most

'Bergmanian' film. With it Tarkovsky literally, at the end of his career, moved into the Swede's territory (at the invitation it should be said not of Bergman himself, but of the Swedish Film Institute, under Anna-Lena Wibom). The film was shot in Gotland, contiguous to the island of Färö (90 or so miles off the Russian coast) where so many of Bergman's own films had been made. Bergman's habitual production team – cinematographer Sven Nykvist, designer Anna Asp, production manager Katinka Faragò – rendered their services willingly. The characters in the film are themselves Swedish, or predominantly so. And even stylistically, for example, in the new penchant for close-up, the film seems to move deliberately towards those middle-period Bergman master-pieces like *The Silence, The Shame* and *Hour of the Wolf*.

Can we push the comparison further? Plainly, Tarkovsky and Bergman, among modern film-makers, share a deep aptitude for metaphysical questioning. But Bergman's atheism is perhaps in the last resort more absolute than Tarkovsky's. God is invoked in Bergman's films only as an absence or nostalgia. At times (as we have noted) Tarkovsky seems scarcely more positive than Berg-man on this; but the measure of friendliness which the Russian shows towards religion, in both his life and his work, is finally a major important difference.

It turns out in fact that one of the sources of *The Sacrifice* is Bergman's film *The Shame* (1969), a work much admired by Tarkovsky (he talks about it in some detail in *Sculpting in Time*). We might go so far as to speculate that Tarkovsky's last work is in some sort an attempted *answer* to the earlier film. *The Shame* (as its title implies) is about man's humiliation in the face of the nuclear threat, whereas *The Sacrifice* is about symbolically facing it.

Can we put this more concretely? *The Shame*, like *The Sacrifice*, envisages at its outset a time of deep nuclear crisis. Local war has already broken out, prelude to the greater devasting holocaust. Liv Ullmann and Max von Sydow play a middle-class couple who have retreated, like Alexander and his family, into the Swedish wilder-ness. The film follows the slowly built-up panic in their souls as they at first stay put, but finally attempt to make a journey out of the battle zone. They do not succeed. The film ends with an image of utter forlorn despair (the couple on a boat in the ocean, surrounded by a drift of floating corpses). It gives us, I think (in comparison to the final liberating shots of *The Sacrifice*), a glimpse of the most characteristic difference between the two artists – a difference of residual religious hope.

We find this most explicitly encountered in either film's attitude towards the future generation. Robin Wood has written about the way in which, in *The Shame*, Liv Ullmann embodies the 'finest humanist maternal instinct'. But the fact is that the couple in *The Shame* are childless. The question of whether children should be brought into the world is one that recurs everywhere in Bergman's cinema. And the grimmest moment in the Liv Ullmann character's psychological demoralisation occurs when she spots a dead little girl (murdered or poisoned by radioactivity) lying on a mossy bank in her nightdress.

Now of course Tarkovsky, too, makes Alexander dream the death of *his* child in *The Sacrifice* (lying bloodstained on a reflecting pane of glass); but I think it important that it only *is* a dream. And one doesn't have to be told, by a closing caption, that *The Sacrifice* is dedicated to Tarkovsky's son Andryusha to see that this is what the whole film is driving at. The child lying at the foot of the tree, and speaking his first muttered words, is plainly the 'redeeming hope'.

Whether the topos arises naturally from the fable, or is imposed unnaturally from without, is the final unanswered question in this great, last, most perplexing of Tarkovsky's films.

TARKOVSKY
PRO AND CONTRA

The films of Tarkovsky are not reticent about their spiritual and religious content. The 'aura of spirituality' in which they and their discussion have been enveloped can be a source of irritation and impatience. Ioseliani, the Georgian director, for example, directs the complaint against Tarkovsky himself: 'It is somewhat ill-bred to be always emphasising how religious you are – it is like boasting that your father is a marquis'* Obviously there are grave matters of taste and tactfulness involved in an artist's coming down on the right side as between true religious feeling and religiosity. Should we, the argument goes, take the clarion cries about the necessity for spirituality at face value? Does the term mean anything authentic? Is it perhaps sanctimonious and unappealing?

The connected criticism is that Tarkovsky's work is egotistic, self-indulgent. Who does he think he is to claim that his private idiosyncratic visions stand for the condition of Russia? And if they do 'stand for' Russia shouldn't he have stayed there and upheld them? According to such a view, there is a sort of moral blindness about Tarkovsky's later actions, not mitigated by his evident artistic genius. Thus Michel Ciment, among critics, is worried about Tarkovsky never truly seeing how elevated and privileged his position was in his homeland. The regime which Tarkovsky abandoned in July 1984 was not condemned in the following press conferences where it should have been – for the manifest civil injustices it displayed towards Tarkovsky's fellow citizens – but exclusively and selfishly because it prevented the artist from following his calling. If we think about it, adds Ciment coolly, six films in 20 years – each fully budgeted – is not in fact such a bad record. (Ioseliani, in the interview just cited, is scornful in a different way: 'Even if the country is poor, and has laws that are difficult to understand, these things are still what make up the life of the land you were born into. So it is better to drink your cup of bitterness – and let's not kid ourselves it's bitter everywhere – in a

*The Times, 27 March 1985, in conversation with David Robinson.

place that is your home, rather than be a foreigner somewhere else'.)

The man and the work are more than usually connected in thinking about Tarkovsky, and a criticism of the one very rapidly becomes a criticism of the other. About the work itself, the films that have been discussed in this book, a number of semi-hostile positions may be maintained. Perhaps what most of them come down to is this: there is a fatal gap in Tarkovsky's work between intellectual concept and communicated feeling. His films are 'over-intellectualised'. They no longer make us weep when they ought to. (Yet I observed many people weeping at the end of *The Sacrifice*.) Konchalovsky, the ex-collaborator of Tarkovsky, now himself forging a successful career in the West, speaks of the crucial difference in Russian culture between the feminine noun *ducha*, meaning heart, and the masculine noun *dukh* meaning mind, implying that in Tarkovsky's case the latter predominates ruinously. And as it predominates (Konchalovsky goes on) so Tarkovsky's films are felt to be lengthy and tedious, increasingly confused in their rhythms and dialogues. An artist who thought he was the open frank Beethoven was in fact more like the esoteric Scriabin.

The preceding chapters will have made essentially clear, I hope, my own position about these charges. At any event, it is certainly true that the admiration, or the dislike, which one harbours for an artist is seldom exclusively limited to the works themselves, but rather extends to a combination of the works and what we sense about the man who lies behind them. Art has an ethical pressure, hand in hand with the aesthetic. The significance of Tarkovsky's films is inevitably (we may agree to this extent with Konchalovsky, Ciment, Ioseliani) bound up with the figure of Tarkovsky himself as a human being. But for me, to meet Tarkovsky was to have the question answered definitively. It was to be in the presence of a certain irreducible human genuineness. There can have been few modern men who so combined courtesy, enthusiasm and high seriousness. The matter and the manner of his speech had a rare harmony, as if, witty and voluble in his opinions, he possessed nonetheless an inner calm – a sort of continuousness of character – that is the mark of a mature human soul.

Of course he was neurotic, like most Russians. As we have said, he was a modern man, post-Dostoevsky, and the suffering expressed in his films' anguished protagonists could be discerned in his own features. But not obtrusively. I harbour memories of his handsome, Asiatic face, dominated by clear, enquiring brown eyes, a face which beautifully combined the traits of masculine forcefulness and feminine sensitivity. Always he spoke with authority, as if words had meaning, and urgency, and were not to be wasted. One occasion, in particular, I remember: he was being interviewed on a public platform at the National Film Theatre. Somehow the meaning of his remarks wasn't coming across. The kindly and yet firm way that Tarkovsky gripped the arm of the interpreter, insisting that he pause and bring out the precise nuance, remains with me as an icon of the seriousness of public human intercourse: talk as it should be, elevated above the plane of triviality.*

Moral strength is difficult to characterise without being prig- gish. The strange attractiveness of Tarkovsky was bound up with the listener's sense of a vulnerability that went hand in hand with his gestural certainty. (The certainty of the film director which, like that of the great concert conductor, issued from a habit of command.) He had an extraordinary inner confidence. Yet his work is about private agonies. It was a particular moral generosity that he didn't see why these should be hidden, either in art or in life. Of course, such self-revelations were all the more impressive in that they emerged from a proud, fastidious and aristocratic human being.

His work is shaped by the sense of the duplicity of human experience – man's capacity for happiness and truth co-existing with a knowledge of loss and imperfection. One sees this most clearly in the attitude which Tarkovsky takes towards death, on the one hand 'abolishing' it magisterially (in the marvellous poems quoted in *The Mirror* and *Nostalghia*); on the other hand, as in *The Sacrifice*, confronting its force as an outrage, dramatising – as no other film artist except Bergman has done – the human fear of death, the 'sickening physical hatred of extinction', death's 'unanswerable' monstruousness and mastery. Tarkovsky's films (the essential ethical sanity of which I have been attempting to bring out all along) are held together by this tragic ambivalence: 'By the time man reaches experience, he is ready to die.'

Tarkovsky's own death, announced as I was finishing this book, makes some of these points allegorical, both because that death was

*A Russian exile of ten years standing tells me that seeing the BBC 'Arena' programme (13 March 1987) and hearing Tarkovsky's voice from the other side of the grave made her, more than any other single incident in the last decade, wish to revisit her homeland.

Tarkovsky directing *Nostalghia* (with Domiziana Giordano)

tragically too soon, but also because of the strange anticipation of it in his earlier work, long before he realised he was afflicted by cancer. Gorchakov's collapse at the end of *Nostalghia* is one such ghostly prevision. So is the death of the modern-day protagonist in *The Mirror*. When, back in 1984, in preparing materials for this study I asked Tarkovsky (by letter) what incidents he had invented for that film he replied: 'Everything happened as I have stated it – except for the scene of the invisible hero's death-bed.' And yet that too was authentic, in retrospect. There is probably only a certain amount that can be said on such a subject. Tarkovsky came to believe, apparently, that the disease he perished from was brought on, at least partially, by the treatment he had received at the hands of the Soviet authorities. (His wife Larissa supports the view.) Of his exile, he wrote bitterly and poignantly in his journal: 'I had to become fatally ill so that I could see my son again.' No one can gauge what agony he suffered in those last months in the clinics of Paris and Germany. What may be said is that his films, by articulating both the horror of death and its place in the overall scheme of things, provide (even for non-believers) a consolation and call towards courage.

A great artist, it is said, creates the taste by which he is judged. The significance of Tarkovsky's effort is naturally impossible to pin down scientifically. But he seems to me above all to have kept alive in the immediate contemporary world the notion that film-making is a high poetic calling. He fought for the position that cinema should engage our concerns as profoundly as literature, painting or music do. (This 'greatest of art forms', he called it, 'of which we are still only learning the secrets.') The decade in which Tarkovsky's work began to emerge in the West, the late 1960s and 1970s, was a curiously transitional time for world film production. The great *auteurs* of the previous decade – Bergman, Antonioni, Bresson, Godard – while still producing and experimenting, had already perhaps done most of their best work. Tarkovsky was the major new figure to emerge. What he brought with him, more than anything else, was a revalidation of personal inner experience over the public dance of politics. His work opens up profoundly different vistas from those suggested by, say, the angry secular radicalism of artists like Godard and Fassbinder. Who, in history's retrospect, will prove to be the most significant director can't be guessed. The grave indifference, veering towards hostility, with which the Russian's work regards Marxism, forces us to re-evaluate, in turn, that period in the late 1960s, when every issue was referable to 'protest'. Tarkovsky's anti-revolutionism is in this sense styptic, and comparable to Solzhenitsyn's: both men professed a similarly decisive rejection.

Which directors, more precisely, Tarkovsky has influenced (and continues to influence) is a question all of its own. Can we take it for example that a film like Edgar Reitz's *Heimat* (1984), where almost for the first time the recent history of Germany is treated non-pathologically (in other words humanely and humanistically), owes something to the spiritual example of Tarkovsky? (The connection seems to me with *The Mirror*.) We sense in Reitz's pioneering work a genuine pushing forward of the boundaries of cinema: an effort towards experimentation (as between documentary and fiction, between colour and black and white, between public and private worlds) which, like Tarkovsky's, is at the furthest possible remove from mere arid formalism.

Elsewhere Tarkovsky's influence may be gauged in the work of certain ambitious new directors attracted as much by the look and texture of his cinema as by its spiritual content and message. (With young directors this is probably to be expected.) Lars Von Trier's *Elements of Crime* (Denmark, 1984), for example, a violent and antinomian police parable, eclectic and obscure, owes its powerful aesthetic conviction to the director having assimilated stylistically, but with a rare degree of intelligence and imagination, the twin cinemas of Tarkovsky and Orson Welles. (His interviews in film reviews endorse an extraordinary admiration for the Russian.)

Similarly we may say that the first film of the talented young New Zealand director Vincent Ward, *Vigil* (1985), is utterly Tarkovskian in its handling of landscape and water. But the influence is legitimate to the extent that it is used to support a world view that is already the director's own, not Tarkovsky's. (It is pessimist, atheist, 'Godforsaken'.) Much the same may be said about the British director Michael Radford (*Another Time, Another Place, Nineteen Eighty-Four*): the influence here is the texture of the image. And let us bring in finally the photography and art direction of a whole school of influential modern British cinema (I am thinking of films from HandMade Productions like Terry Gilliam's *Time Bandits*, 1981, and *Brazil*, 1984).

Thus there are stylistic influences on the one hand; more complex emotional influences on the other. Tarkovsky's own 'handwriting' is unforgeable, but there is evidently something about him that other younger artists find congenial. In an age in which televisual and filmic images are becoming, in their blandness, harder and harder to disentangle, Tarkovsky's cinema stands as a beacon and beckoning point. The richness and density of his vision serve as a reminder (for backsliders) and a confirmation (for cinephiles) of the continuing majesty of cinema.

APPENDIX: Vicissitudes of *Andrei Roublev*

The story of *Andrei Roublev*'s famous troubles I find to be one of those parables whose moral remains hauntingly elusive. For on the one hand there is an attested obstructionism on the part of the Russian authorities, causing the film-maker, over a number of years, grief, anger, frustration. On the other hand there is a grudging honourableness – maybe no more than a residual respect for legality – which determined that, a contract with the West having being signed (foolishly, as they later thought), the film would eventually have to be shown. (Still, without the sustained presence of critical opinion set up by friends of the film-maker outside Russia, who knows what that 'eventually' might have turned into?)

The facts are now somewhat distant, but the chronology seems approximately to have been this. The earliest Western request to exhibit the film came from the committee of the Venice festival, who had honoured *Ivan's Childhood*, early in 1966. They were told – which was true at the time – that the film was 'still being completed'. (It was finished later that year, in August.) The following year Venice tried again and were given the same answer, this time with possibly less good faith. Meanwhile Favre Le Bret of the Cannes festival had seen a copy of the film in Moscow early in 1967, had been immensely impressed, and made a request for the film at his festival (to take place in May 1967). The answer now was that there were 'technical difficulties' and he too ought to try again next year.

In the summer of 1967, an international study seminar at Repino near Leningrad brought domestic disagreement about the film out into the open. Despite qualified praise from certain brave journalists, the film was officially condemned in newspapers and magazines for cruelty, naturalism, anti-patriotism and 'religiosity'. Requests were made for quite severe cuts, which Tarkovsky (protected by copyright) obstinately refused.

1968 was frustrating for Tarkovsky. It was the year of Prague, the year of student unrest, cancellations and disruptions at the major Western film festivals, a darkening of relations between East and West. Yet at the same time, by what must later have seemed an amazing oversight, a Western distribution company, Promeco (representing Columbia Pictures), acquired rights from Goskino and Sovexport for the film's distribution in twenty-two foreign countries.

1969 seems to have been in many ways the key year for the film's fortunes. It started with Le Bret, this time with the backing of the French Communist Party, making another request to show the film at Cannes. He was told that it would be permitted, but only for the unofficial section (and only if it appeared without the logo 'The USSR presents ...'). There was then much jostling and politicking about when the film would be screened at Cannes (the Soviet authorities naturally wanted it as late as possible, after the prizes had been awarded). The first screening in the West, finally, was at 4 a.m. on the festival's last day, under the logo of the 'Union of Soviet Film-makers'. Out of running of course for the main prize, *Andrei Roublev* was immediately awarded the International Critics' (FIPRESCI) Prize: a large part of the 20-member jury, incidentally, came from the Eastern bloc countries. It was agreed that the plaque would be handed over to Tarkovsky at the Moscow Film Festival in July.

News of the prize infuriated the authorities in Moscow. Brezhnev apparently demanded a screening of the film, and made his feelings clear by walking out in the middle. The powerful bureaucrat Suslov saw it too, and pronounced his own private veto. Thus the Moscow festival passed in an atmosphere of tension and ideological obstructionism – the award ceremony for Tarkovsky being put off from day to day, finally to some 'indefinite time in the future'. Requests for private viewings of the film by Western journalists were refused.

It was now clear that the authorities wished the film never to be shown again in public. Goskino put pressure on the agreement with Columbia, who backed down (at least temporarily). One independent distributor in France, however, held out. This company had a legally acquired print of the film which they held on to determinedly, despite every effort of the Soviet Embassy (at both the highest government level and the lowest level of intrigue) to retrieve it. It was probably the showing of this print throughout 1970 in the Paris cinemas that finally and happily determined the film's fate, as public pressure built up everywhere to have the film released properly. Making the best of a bad job (there was also the foreign currency angle to think of), the Soviet authorities finally, in October 1971, gave way.

Yet as Elem Klimov remarked (when asked by the author about the incident at a 1987 National Film Theatre interview), Goskino made sure that throughout the rest of the 1970s such a mistake was never made again.

FILMOGRAPHY

Andrei Tarkovsky was born in Zavrozhne, north of Moscow, on 4 April 1932. After studying Arabic and working briefly as a geologist, he enrolled at the state cinema institute (VGIK) in Moscow, where in 1959 he made a short film, *There Will Be No Leave Today*. His diploma film was *The Steamroller and the Violin*. From 1983 Tarkovsky lived abroad. He died in Paris on 29 December 1986.

Abbreviations
P.c.   Production company
P.   Producer
D.   Director
Sc.   Screenplay
Ph.   Photography
Ed.   Editor
A.d.   Art Director
M.   Music
Sd.   Sound

1960   **Katok i skrypka** (The Steamroller and the Violin)
P.c: Mosfilm (Children's Film Unit). D: Andrei Tarkovsky. Sc: Andrei Tarkovsky, Andrei Mikhalkov Konchalovsky. Ph: Vadim Yusev (Sovcolor). Ed: L. Butuzova. A.d: S. Agoyan. M: Vyacheslav Ovchinnikov. Sd: V. Krachkovsky.
Igor Fomchenko *(Sasha)*, V. Zamansky *(Sergei)*, N. Arkhangelskaya *(Girl)*, Marina Adzhubei *(Mother)*, Yura Brusev, Slava Borisev, Sasha Vitoslavsky, Sasha Ilin, Kolya Kozarev, Zhenya Klyachkovsky, Igor Kolovikov, Zhenya Fedochenko, Tanya Prokhorova, A. Maximova, L. Semyonova, G. Zhdanova, M. Figner.
46 mins.

1962   **Ivanovo Detstvo** (Ivan's Childhood)
P.c: Mosfilm. D: Andrei Tarkovsky. Sc: Mikhail Papava, Vladimir Bogomolov. Based on the novella *Ivan* by V. Bogomolov. Ph: Vadim Yusev. Ed: G. Natanson. A.d: Evgeny Chernyaev. M: Vyacheslav Ovchinnikov. Sd: E. Zelentsova.
Nikolai Burlyaev *(Ivan)*, Valentin Zubkov *(Capt. Kholin)*, E. Zharikov *(Lt. Galtsev)*, S. Krylov *(Sgt. Katasonov)*, V. Malyavina *(Masha)*, Nikolai Grinko *(Col. Grazhnev)*, D. Milyutenko *(Old man with hen)*,

Irina Tarkovskaya *(Ivan's Mother)*, Andrei Mikhalkov Konchalovsky *(Soldier with spectacles)*, Ivan Savkin, V. Marenkov, Vera Miturich. 95 mins.

1966 Andrei Roublev

P.c: Mosfilm. D: Andrei Tarkovsky. Sc: Andrei Mikhalkov Konchalovsky, Andrei Tarkovsky. Ph: Vadim Yusev (Scope, part in Sovcolor). Ed. Ludmila Feyganova. A.d: Evgeny Chernyaev. M: Vyacheslav Ovchinnikov. Sd: E. Zelentsova.

Anatoly Solonitsin *(Andrei Roublev)*, Ivan Lapikov *(Kyril)*, Nikolai Grinko *(Daniel the Black)*, Nikolai Sergeyev *(Theophanes the Greek)*, Irina Tarkovskaya *(Deaf-and-dumb girl)*, Nikolai Burlyaev *(Boriska)*, Rolan Bykov *(Buffoon)*, Yuri Nikulin *(Patrikey)*, Mikhail Kononov *(Fomka)*, Yuri Nazarov *(Grand Duke/His brother)*, S. Krylov *(Bellfounder)*, Sos Sarkissian *(The Christ)*, Bolot Eishelanev *(Tartar chief)*, N. Grabbe, B. Beishenaliev, B. Matisik, A. Obukhov, Volodya Titov. 186 mins.

1972 Solaris

P.c: Mosfilm. D: Andrei Tarkovsky. Sc: Andrei Tarkovsky, Friedrich Gorenstein. Based on the novel by Stanislaw Lem. Ph: Vadim Yusev (Scope, Sovcolor). Ed: Ludmila Feyganova. A.d: Mikhail Romadin. M: Eduard Artemyev; Chorale prelude in F min. by J. S. Bach.

Donatas Banionis *(Kris Kelvin)*, Natalya Bondarchuk *(Hari)*, Yuri Jarvet *(Snauth)*, Anatoly Solonitsin *(Sartorius)*, Vladislav Dvorzhetsky *(Burton)*, Nikolai Grinko *(Father)*, Sos Sarkissian *(Gibaryan)*, O. Yisilova *(Kelvin's mother)*. 165 mins.

1974 Zerkalo (The Mirror)

P.c: Mosfilm. D: Andrei Tarkovsky. Sc: Andrei Tarkovsky, Aleksandr Misharin. Ph: Georgy Rerberg (Sovcolor, part in black and white). Ed: Ludmila Feyganova. A.d: Nikolai Dvigubsky. Sets: A. Merkulov. M: Eduard Artemyev; extracts from Pergolesi, Purcell, J. S. Bach. Sd: Semyon Litvinov. Narrator: Innokenti Smoktunovsky. Arseny Tarkovsky's poems read by himself.

Margarita Terekhova *(Mother/Natalia)*, Philip Yankovsky *(Ignat at 5)*, Ignat Daniltsev *(Ignat at 12)*, Oleg Yankovsky *(Father)*, Nikolai Grinko *(Man at printers)*, Alla Demidova *(Lisa)*, Yuri Nazarov *(Military instructor)*, Anatoly Solonitsin *(Passer-by)*, L. Tarkovskaya *(Alexei's mother as an old woman)*, Tamara Ogorodnikova, Y. Sventikov, T. Reshetnikova, E. del Bosque, L. Correcher, A. Gutierrez, D. Garcia, T. Pames, Teresa del Bosque, Tatiana del Bosque. 106 mins.

1979 **Stalker**
P.c. Mosfilm. D: Andrei Tarkovsky. Sc: Arkady Strugatsky, Boris Strugatsky. Based on their story *Roadside Picnic*. Ph: Aleksandr Knyazhinsky (colour). Ed: Ludmila Feyganova. A.d: Andrei Tarkovsky. Sets: A. Merkulov. M: Eduard Artemyev. Sd: V. Sharun.
Alexander Kaidanovsky *(Stalker)*, Anatoly Solonitsin *(Writer)*, Nikolai Grinko *(Scientist)*, Alissa Freindlikh *(Stalker's wife)*, Natasha Abramova, F. Yurna, E. Kostin, R. Rendi.
161 mins.

1983 **Nostalghia**
P.c: Opera Film. For Rete 2 TV RAI (Rome)/Sovin Film (Moscow). P: Francesco Casati. D: Andrei Tarkovsky. Sc: Andrei Tarkovsky, Tonino Guerra. Ph: Giuseppe Lanci (Eastman Colour). Ed: Erminia Marani, Amedeo Salfa. A.d: Andrea Crisanti. M. adviser: Gino Peguri. Sd: Remo Ugolinelli. Sd. effects: Luciano Anzellotti, Massimo Anzellotti.
Oleg Yankovsky *(Andrei Gorchakov)*, Domiziana Giordano *(Evgenia)*, Erland Josephson *(Domenico)*, Patrizia Terreno *(Gorchakov's wife)*, Laura De Marchi *(Woman with towel)*, Delia Boccardo *(Domenico's wife)*, Milena Vukotic *(Municipal employee)*, Alberto Canepa *(Peasant)*, Raffaele Di Mario, Rate Furlan, Livio Galassi, Piero Vida, Elena Magoia.
126 mins.

1986 **Offret** (The Sacrifice)
P.c: Swedish Film Institute (Stockholm)/Argos Films (Paris). In association with Film Four International, Josephson & Nykvist, Sveriges Television/SVT2, Sandrew Film & Teater. With the participation of the French Ministry of Culture. Exec. p: Anna-Lena Wibom. P: Katinka Faragò. D: Andrei Tarkovsky. Sc: Andrei Tarkovsky. Ph: Sven Nykvist (Eastman Colour, part in black and white). Ed: Andrei Tarkovsky, Michal Leszczylowski. A.d: Anna Asp. M: 'St. Matthew Passion' by J. S. Bach; Swedish and Japanese folk music. Sd: Owe Svensson, Bosse Persson, Lars Ulander, Christin Loman, Wikee Peterson-Berger.
Erland Josephson *(Alexander)*, Susan Fleetwood *(Adelaide)*, Valérie Mairesse *(Julia)*, Allan Edwall *(Otto)*, Gudrún Gisladóttir *(Maria)*, Sven Wollter *(Victor)*, Filippa Franzén *(Marta)*, Tommy Kjellqvist *(Little Man)*, Per Kallman and Tommy Nordahl *(Ambulancemen)*.
149 mins.

Tarkovsky was artistic adviser on *Terpkig Vinograd* (1973, directed by Bagrat Organisian), and wrote the script for *Beregis! Zmej* (1979). According to François Albera (*Positif* no. 310, December 1986), Tarkovsky also wrote or contributed to the scripts of *The First Teacher* (1965, directed by A. Mikhalkov Konchalovsky), *A Chance in a Thousand*

(1965, directed by L. Katcharian, A. Mikhalkov Konchalovsky), *The End of Ataman* (1971, directed by Ayimanov), *Tashkent, City of Plenty* (1969, directed by Abbasov), and *The Ferocious One* (1973, directed by Okeyev).

Tarkovsky's projects included film versions of *Hamlet, The Idiot, The Temptations of St Anthony*, and a film about the life of E.T.A. Hoffmann (*Hoffmanniana*).

Tarkovsky directed *Hamlet* at the Komsomol Theatre in Leningrad in 1977; and Mussorgsky's opera *Boris Godunov* at Covent Garden, London in 1983.

The Italian director Donatella Baglivo made three films about Tarkovsky: *Meeting Mr Tarkovsky* (1982), *Andrei Tarkovsky directs 'Nostalghia'* (1983), and *Andrei Tarkovsky, the story of a poet* (1984), all available from CIAK, 167 Circonvallazione Clodia, Rome. A BBC TV 'Arena' programme (13 March 1987) was devoted to Tarkovsky, and a documentary, *Behind the Scenes on 'The Sacrifice'*, was broadcast on Channel Four in early 1987.

BIBLIOGRAPHICAL NOTE

A personal list, by no means exhaustive, of words which I have found helpful would have to start with Tarkovsky's own meditations on cinema *Sculpting in Time* (Bodley Head, 1986, new American ed. 1987). The book is in certain ways clumsily written, and on occasions obscure. But it contains on the other hand so many profound and striking aperçus, such a depth of simple ethical wisdom, that I am inclined to argue that it is one of the best general film books in any sphere that has come out in the past twenty years. Mention too (although on a lesser plane) ought to be made of another study that I have at times found extremely useful, *A. T: Film als Poesie, Poesie als Film* (Keil Verlag, Bonn, 1981) by an early collaborator of Tarkovsky, M. J. Turovskaya. (It is being translated and will be published by Faber & Faber.)

The standard English-language book on Russian cinema is *Kino* by Jay Leyda (1960, 3rd ed. 1983), though Leyda's judgments are not always mine. (Cinema, more almost than any other art form, has a constantly evolving history, changing fascinatingly as more and more films become available from the archives.) A clear, well-documented book in French with excellent illustrations is *Le Cinéma Russe et Soviétique* edited by J. L. Passek (Centre Georges Pompidou, 1981). On the great central figures of Soviet film history – Eisenstein, Pudovkin, Dovzhenko, Dziga Vertov etc. – no one is more provocative than the film historian Herbert Marshall, whose *Masters of Soviet Cinema : Crippled Creative Biographies* (Routledge & Kegan Paul, 1983) provides, with occasional extravagance, indispensable biographical insight. I have found Marie Seton's biography of *Eisenstein*, because so partisan and personal, extremely illuminating (Dobson, revised ed. 1978). Barthélemy Amengual has written an exemplary poetic short text on *Dovzhenko* (Seghers, 1979), supplemented now by the scholarly work of the American historian Vance Kepley (*The Cinema of Dovzhenko*, University of Wisconsin Press, 1986). The early heroic years of Russian cinema are sociologically investigated by Richard Taylor in *The Politics of Soviet Cinema 1917–1929* (Cambridge University Press, 1979). As supplement or alternative to this, a booklet containing interesting early texts has been published by the British Film Institute: *Futurism, Formalism, FEKS: 'Eccentrism' and the Soviet Cinema 1918–36*, edited by Ian Christie and John Gillett (revised edition 1987). Two English-language, Russian-published film encyclopaedias can be mentioned. *The Phenomenon of the Soviet Cinema* by Yuri Vorontsev (Progress Publishers, 1980) is dully written but contains an extensive alphabetical filmography; *Who's Who in the Soviet Cinema*, on the other hand, by Galina Dolmatovskaya and Irina Shilova (Progress Publishers, 1979), is delightful — excellently composed portraits (seventy in all) of Russian actors and directors.

So far as the general cultural background of Russia in the 20th century is concerned, of course the subject is vast and no sensible bibliography would aim to cover all of it. My own thoughts on these matters come from a number of sources, some of which are: Pasternak, whose *Doctor Zhivago* (Collins Harvill, 1958) I read long ago and continue to admire greatly; Solzhenitsyn (*The Oak and the Calf*, Fontana, 1980 – incomparable insights into literary production in the 1950s and 1960s); and, more recently, the memoirs of the opera singer Galina Vishnevskaya (*Galina*, Hodder, 1985). In this context too should be mentioned the extra-ordinary prison-and-exile documents, surely among the great works of literature in the 20th century: *As I Remember Them* by Galina von Meck (Dobson, 1973), *Hope Against Hope* and *Hope Abandoned* by Nadezhda Mandelstam (Collins, 1971, 1974), *Into the Whirlwind* and *Within the Whirlwind* by Evgenia Ginzburg (Collins, 1967, 1981). I have found Norman Stone's essay on Russia in the pre-Revolutionary period compellingly argued (*Europe Transformed, 1878–1919*, Fontana, 1983); while Geoffrey Hosking's general students' history (*A History of the Soviet Union*, Fontana, 1985) is informative and well written.

Back with Tarkovsky himself, the clearest statements about him and by him have appeared in various film journals. There is a wealth of material in the two Parisian magazines, *Positif* and *Cahiers du Cinéma*. I should mention from *Positif*, firstly, Michel Ciment's pioneering interview with A. T. about *Andrei Roublev* (issue 109, October 1969); also subsequent dossiers and extensive interviews in issues 247 (October 1981), 249 (December 1981), 284 (October 1984), 303 and 304 (May and June 1986) and 312 (February 1987). (Emmanuel Carrère and Petr Kral are among the first-rate contributing essayists.) In addition there are excellent articles on the more recent Russian cinema in issue 310 (December 1986). *Cahiers du Cinéma* came late to Tarkovsky, but they have somewhat made up for it by publishing extensive dossiers in issues 358 (April 1984), 386 (July-August 1986) and 392 (February 1987), all useful. In Britain the veteran magazine *Sight and Sound* has been a long-time supporter of Tarkovsky's work: Ivor Montagu's 1973 article 'Man and Experience: Tarkovsky's World' (vol. 42, no. 2, Spring 1973) still reads well; Herbert Marshall's essay on *The Mirror* (vol. 45, no. 2, Spring 1976) has already been mentioned in the text, as has Peter Green's essay on *Stalker* (vol. 54, no. 1, Winter 1984–5); but not this latter writer's equally carefully argued article on *The Sacrifice* (vol. 56, no. 2, Spring 1987). Excellent interviews by Angus McKinnon and Chris Auty may be found in back issues of the London listings magazine *Time Out*: nos. 568 (6 March 1981), 686 (17 November 1981) and 729 (9 August 1984). *The Listener* of 23 August 1984 reprints the broadcast which Tarkovsky gave on the Russian service of the BBC after his decision to stay in the West.

I should mention finally a short collection of essays edited by Michel Estève in *Etudes Cinématographiques* (special issue 135–138, Paris, 1983); and a little Italian book, *Andrej Tarkovskij*, edited by Sandro Petraglia (Edizioni A.I.A.C.E., Turin, 1975), with much rare information, parti-cularly about the distribution fortunes of *Andrei Roublev*.

INDEX